THE TWO-EDGED SWORD

A Study of the Paranoid Personality in Action

THE
TWO-EDGED
SWORD

A Study of the Paranoid Personality in Action

by
William H. Hampton, M.D.
and
Virginia Schroeder Burnham

SUNDIAL
PUBLICATIONS

First Edition

Printed in the United States of America

Library of Congress Cataloging in Publication Data:

Hampton, William H., 1925-
        The two-edged sword : a study of the paranoid personality in
    action / by William H. Hampton and Virginia Schroeder Burnham. --
    1st ed.
            p.   cm.
        ISBN: 0-86534-147-8 : $14.95
        1. Paranoia. I. Burnham, Virginia Schroeder, 1908-
    II. Title.
        RC520.H35 1990
        616.89'7--dc20   90-37-97
                                                                        CIP

Published in 1990 by SUNSTONE PRESS
                Post Office Box 2321
            Santa Fe, NM 87504-2321 / USA

CONTENTS

FOREWORD

T his book is to aid us in a deeper comprehension of what we are and to bring comfort to our sense of self. As the Bard of Avon said: "There is nothing either good or bad, but thinking makes it so." (Hamlet II, ii) Human thinking can elevate us above the beast, or it can submerge us far beneath. The thinking makes the difference. So here is an intensive look at a sphere of human brain function that may well explain the heights and depths of the human condition—a human brain function known as paranoid mentation.

Paranoid thinking, you say, "I know what that is—suspicion and anger, delusions, and voices whispering threats, assault and revenge—Caesar and Hitler and Manson." Yes, you have the idea. But there is more, much more. Because paranoia is not just extremism, not just psychosis, not just abnormality. Paranoia is also safety, sanity, and normal when we are in danger. Paranoia galvanizes, stimulates and fuels our competitive natures. Paranoia gives our leaders their motivation and guidance. Paranoia is in all of us, some of us strongly and some of us weakly. But we have it and we need to know what it is and what it does to us. Because paranoia will run our lives if we don't catch on to its secret power. Then we can direct our lives and balance our emotions.

"Hey, Rube!", calls the carnival man, seeking help from his working mates. Modern psychiatry calls on us to help ourselves. We call on you to know your paranoid self so you can help yourself. Without the insight and inner direction that this knowledge gives, you are vulnerable and beset by tremendous forces generated by the emotions. And paranoid emotion is the controlling, combative, competitive drive that fuels the emotional center of your nervous machinery.

The science of the brain is reaching into this hitherto mysterious nervous function. We know now so much of the neuro-chemistry of the mental mechanism that we are within reach of comprehending what occurs in our thinking process. However, we still need to develop a total overview of the mind. This requires a greater analysis than just chemistry. As Osler said, "Mix the oil of science with the water of art."

So we present here our vision of what our mental function is with a focus on that special process known as paranoid mentation. Our hope is that you will use this book as a tool to develop your self knowledge and self control. Your improved insight and management will permit you to examine and develop potential that may be blocked, but is soon to be freed from the chains of ignorance. Then you will be in tune with yourself.

Let the "music of the spheres" sing through your life with this new revelation.

William H. Hampton, M.D.
Greenwich, Connecticut
1990

PREFACE

Paranoia, a characteristic we all share, is a valuable and necessary constituent of personality—part of the drive toward self-preservation. "Paranoia" is perhaps the most misunderstood word of its kind in common use. Most of us equate it with excessive fear and distrust of others; but this is only one extreme portion of this complex quality. Everyone is paranoid, or should be, when it comes to his physical, mental, and emotional well-being. If one has too little paranoia, he or she may be extremely naive, immature and susceptible to control by others. Those who are overly paranoid are generally aggressive, demanding, controlling, and extremely difficult to live with. But they may well be successful in managerial roles; as corporate executives, or political and religious leaders. Their compulsion to control, manipulate, and acquire may result in the accumulation of great wealth or power, but extreme paranoia alone is not sufficient to guarantee this. High energy and/or intelligence are also required. Many highly paranoid people never achieve their goals because they lack the latter qualities. Paranoids of this type often end up living behind the triple-locked doors of homes from which they rarely venture on account of the dangers "outside." Most of us fall between these two extremes.

How do we relate to these three basic personality types? In general, highly paranoid people are the least comfortable to be with because of their demanding and controlling natures. Yet often others turn to them for advice and support, because of their confident and overbearing manner. The least paranoid person is apt to be naive and inept, but likable and non-threatening—someone you readily warm up to. The moderately paranoid majority may well be the most successful in terms of self-esteem, lasting relationships, slow but steady contributions to society, and personal growth in self-realization.

Two of the four cornerstones of personality are the qualities of "thinking" and "doing." The paranoid tendency may take root in both the contemplative and the activist, but with different outcomes. The reflective person often turns his paranoid qualities into benevolent channels, while more aggressive personality types usually inflict their hostility and distrust on everyone around them.

This book suggests how you can identify paranoia in yourself and others and discriminate between healthy self-protective attitudes and unhealthy extremes that affect you adversely. It offers insight into dealing with the excessively paranoid people whom we inevitably meet in daily life, and hopefully, shows that well-meaning efforts to change such people are almost certain to fail. We may love them or leave them, depending upon our own emotional needs, but they are well armored against the kind of vulnerability that comes with steadfast attachments and a quiet fidelity to one's chosen course in life.

PARANOIA AND YOU 1

What is paranoia? It is a personality trait common to all living things—from plants to insects to human beings. A two-edged sword, both protective and destructive. Its influence is pervasive and enters into much of what we think and do. Paranoia is a combination of emotions, one of which is an awareness of an extreme and sensitive type with emphasis on self-protection, resulting in fearful suspicion.

The paranoia in our personalities benefits the human race, yet tries to destroy it. So it's both good and bad, but has helped human beings evolve into the modern, social animals of today—both a blessing and a danger. Paranoia has promoted and yet restricted our evolution in the development of the family, communities and nations. It was part of the process by which human beings progressed from a primitive to a cultured civilized state. Paranoia is also responsible for the evolution of politics, religions, war, peace, science, and technology. It has been recognized since Hippocrates.

Most people think of paranoia as one-faceted—morbid fear. But it's more than that. In an excessive, exaggerated form, however, it is a sickness, but in the right amount, it allows humanity to operate smoothly. Too much is destructive, and too little is also destructive. However, we need some in order to survive.

Although paranoia is inborn, the amount varies from person to person. What is the right amount? That's difficult to judge, for paranoia is so intricately interwoven into the fabric of personality it's impossible to evaluate it independently. Paranoia is like a sixth sense, always present and coloring everything you think and do. It has many images, one is being afraid of physical harm, and provides the suspicious, apprehensive, wary quality so necessary for self-protection. So it protects you, warms and enfolds you, and makes you self-critical, courageous, careful, and cautiously defensive. It brings out your gossipy and deceitful features that make you blame another when things go wrong. And it's being assured and self-centered, at times with no regard for the needs of others—your selfish element.

Paranoia drives you to manipulate others so you can control them, especially those close to you, and to control situations, whether or not you have the right. This makes you feel "all powerful." In the paranoid mind, control equals safety. Paranoia doesn't let you accept criticism, yet lets you criticize others.

Most people think to be paranoid is to be afraid. That's true, but it's much more. It makes you alert but suspicious, observant but critical, intelligent but unreasoning. It's the part of your personality that is hard to live with, yet can't live without. When you experience these emotions, your paranoia is at work.

Do you sometimes feel unfriendly and antagonistic but don't know why? Do you suspect the motives of a stranger? Your paranoia is at work. All living things react to fear in a manner called the "fight or flight" syndrome. It is a primitive emotion and paranoia enhances it, and when you are caught in a crisis, you react in one of two ways. You fight or run away. As you quickly decide which course to take, your paranoia protects you.

Let's talk about John Doakes, who has a lot of paranoia. John doesn't trust anyone and is fearful of things that don't bother you or me. He's afraid he'll be attacked, physically or verbally, so he's constantly on the alert. He feels that others are ganging up to strike out at him. Sometimes, he jumps the gun and takes the offensive without provocation. His high paranoia supersedes his better judgment. Other people can't understand him and don't accept his action. Rejection intensifies his paranoia, and he distrusts others without reason and blames them when something goes wrong. He is highly suspicious and questions the kindest motives. His paranoia gives rise to unrealistic anxiety and insecurity. He is not a happy man.

On the other hand Jane Doakes has too little paranoia. She is naive, unworldly and trusting, so she is vulnerable to emotional onslaughts, exploitation and even fraud. She is apt to trust all people, is not afraid and sometimes takes foolish risks. "Friends" use her and take advantage of her. She is trying to develop more paranoia to protect herself better.

And what does paranoia do for you and me and Tim Dolan with an average amount? It fuels our energy systems in mind and body and gives us the ability to choose a course of action and act on it. It motivates us to go after resources and interests that are good, such as the control of self, relationships with others, security in life, and sexual satisfaction. Low paranoids give passively in the sexual area and are apt to be indiscriminate and guilty, those with more paranoia are discriminate but take all they can get without guilt because they desire to control their feelings. Thus, the average paranoids have a healthy way, with recognition and acceptance of control, guilt and a fair return for the effort put into life.

You can apply these concepts to yourself, by studying how you react to life situations and thus determine the degree of paranoid drive you possess. It influences everything you think and do, from relationships with your family, loved ones and friends to your sex life. It is a guiding light for your dealings with others, tempered by your thinking and doing qualities. It is intimately entwined with your love for those you hold dear and interests about which you feel strongly. It applies to your work, if and how you make money, and how you use that money.

So you see how valuable your paranoid quality is and how important to learn to control it and use it to your advantage. If it controls you, it can carry you into hostile areas and ruin your life. Your paranoia takes care of your needs when you use it properly. It takes care of your innermost feelings, your curious mind, your sexual drive and your search for security. It directs you to your need for family, and the material acquisitions to be comfortable, your sexual conquests, the need for companionship, and competition. So the major drive of paranoia is control of your life and future—this is its essence.

The elements of security and personal satisfaction hinge on your paranoia. This applies to people with an average degree, but if you are one with less, work on enriching the little you have and it will stand you in good stead. People take advantage of someone like you, so be wary and think twice before you trust. You won't be hurt so much. Therefore, enhance your paranoid thinking by being more suspicious, more controlling, more hostile and more demanding. If you have more than average paranoia, you may be an unpleasant person, difficult and challenging, but probably not dangerously so. People don't like you and seem to avoid you. If this bothers you, smother your paranoia and let someone else control. Only you can increase or decrease it by being aware of your thoughts and actions.

As a good Christian, or Jew or Moslem, are your feelings and thoughts consistent with what you believe? And do you apply what you believe to what you do? This is very difficult because the paranoid element gets in the way. The need to satisfy yourself is such an overriding concern that even as a religious person, it is impossible for you to go halves with another, whether it is a business deal or a golf match or any competition. You always want the largest share. Your drive to succeed and control supersedes all considerations.

How can I identify a paranoid trend in me? Will it suddenly show up and start to run me? It shows up when you are threatened, or hurt, or sick, or in pain, but it can't happen if you are aware and recognize it. It also appears when you are in trouble. Then, you're more suspicious, hostile and aggressive and more interested in self, so you become defensive and able to take action. This is paranoia protecting you. It is temporary, however, and soon calms down and goes into its niche to lie quietly until it's needed again. Therefore, we all have a little or more or a lot, and need it for protection.

In general, the more paranoia you have the more prosperous you will be, but not well-liked; the less you have the nicer person you will be, but not as successful. So look at yourself and pick out your paranoid thoughts. The stronger they are the more controlling you will try to be, so watch it. The weaker, the more ineffectual, so try to reinforce it. You can't change the amount you were born with, but with insight and sel knowledge, you can draw on that pool of resources that makes up your personality, so you control it and it doesn't control you. Knowledge is power over paranoia, not changing it in amount but in the effect on your life.

Before we go further, let's describe the makeup of personality. A personality has four cornerstones: the "thinking" and the "doing", which go hand in hand, plus "intelligence" and "energy," or "drive." These form the foundation, and the type of personality is determined by the predominance of thinking or of doing, influenced by intelligence and energy. In addition, there are passive and aggressive traits and obsessive and compulsive feelings which stay in the background until a situation forces them into use. Then there is the quality of paranoia which is so difficult to distinguish from the others. Paranoia influences every thought and act, which is thinking and doing, and is intricately involved with them in an inscrutable fashion.

These characteristics of personality are not inherited from parents, or even grandparents. Rather, a personality is made up of genes going back many generations. perhaps over thousands of years. Hence, a person is essentially different from his parents, as his children are from him, although they may have traits in common. Every personality embodies some degree of every characteristic known to man. They differ in degree in each individual and don't change through life. However, education, experience, and the environment play a part in modifying, enhancing or repressing them.

The thinking and doing are balanced, making one hundred percent, and are closely related, each struggling for control, shifting from more thinking to less doing, then more doing and less thinking, until finally when at rest, settling down to their basic amounts. No one can function without them, as they are dependent on one another and helpless when separated. Thus, you can't move without thinking, and when you think, you plan some sort of doing, such as writing, walking, or speaking. This causes activity within your brain cells, which have chemical and electrical components—thinking stimulated by the chemical and doing by the electrical.

Thinking is the internal working of the brain and doing the external. Most problems come from efforts to coordinate the two. A person has some, but not total control. The thinking side is sensitive, introverted and idealistic. It likes creative activities: painting, designing, writing, engineering, building. It's the quality that wants to be alone, to read and study and create, and to focus on details. It's the mathematical part that is oriented toward objects. Predominantly thinking persons relate to things more easily than to people and enjoy using their minds. They are not people persons, as doing persons are.

The doing element is involved whenever a person moves, as the brain communicates with the muscles through nerves. Doing is the acting out trait which is essentially living—everything a person does, and every move he makes. The doing person deals more easily with people than with things. It's the element that loves excitement—the happy-go-lucky, gregarious, extroverted, fun-loving part, that is visible to the world and influences action. The predominant doer is a pleasure-oriented person; he loves to mix with people and chooses a career that involves interpersonal relations, such as selling, directing, politics, administration.

Those who commit crimes have an excessive amount of the doing element, plus poor judgment and a lack of moral instinct. They don't learn by being jailed, and when released, return to the streets to resume the same lifestyle. So the public continues to be threatened by drug addicts, vandals, thieves, muggers and murderers. Up until the last fifty years, these criminals were banned from society. Now we try to preserve all kinds, and seem more willing to tolerate them than to pay the taxes needed to incarcerate them. Hopefully, this will change.

Not all extreme doers are criminals, however, but all have a tendency to disregard the feelings of others. They don't care if they hurt you and can't understand why you're upset when they do. They have no sympathy, and ride roughshod over others, leaving behind them a trail of unhappiness. They make poor parents and worse marriages, as they have little understanding. They give the impression of indifference, and extreme paranoia intensifies these traits.

So, each personality is unique, has never been duplicated and never will be—no two people are exactly alike, not even identical twins. Personality is a heritage that doesn't change and remains through life. This individuality is a law of nature and applies to all forms of life, whether animals, flowers, trees or snowflakes.

HOW DO YOU RECOGNIZE PARANOIA? 2

Paranoia is primitive and obvious in animals. Touch a sleeping dog and he instantly wakes up. That is paranoia, self-protec tive and raw. It is his defense. Watch a bird at the bird feeder. He lights and looks about before he eats. If a squirrel comes, he flies away, or if there is a noise from the house or he sees you, he takes off. Why? Because there is a moment when he is not protected, so he quickly picks up a seed and flies to the top of a tree where he can eat in safety. These expressions of paranoia are good. Ninety-nine times out of a hundred they are not necessary, but the hundredth time the bird's life is saved.

My cats are good examples. One is overly paranoid and the other not paranoid enough. When a stranger comes to the house, Gappy disappears into the cellar, while Pywacket marches into the room, sniffs at the guest's leg, jumps onto a chair and goes to sleep. Paranoia as a defense mechanism is not as efficient in humans, nor is it as effective in domestic animals as in wild. A human being's paranoia is of a cerebral nature—more thinking. The animal's response is physical—more doing.

The human race has evolved in a way that has produced more paranoia, and we see more today because those with a lot survived over time and many of those with little did not. The history of man tells us that the most suspicious people always seemed to prosper. That is why we have the "me" generation: those with a strong desire to get what they want. This should have been tempered, but society failed by condoning and giving in to it. But basically, it is a healthy need, and is not sick, as most people think. However, it is a danger if it grows too strong.

Presidents of large corporations are examples; they got there because of high paranoia. They may be selfdirected and aggressive, but it's a healthy aggression. Although they may not be popular, they are valuable to their companies, and they will create waves and come out on top because of that aggressive, controlling drive to succeed. Thus, the person with little paranoia puts aside his need; the one with moderate at times allows the other person the upper hand, and the xtreme paranoid strives to win in a business deal, a political setting, religious milieu and usually in marriage and personal relationships.

They are so compelled to satisfy themselves, get their way and control the situation that they work harder, have less concern for others and always try to get a bigger share of the pie.

Such persons are universally disliked; there is consistent antagonism toward them, to which they pay little attention and may use to manipulate criticism into a compliment. For instance, a man with high paranoia comes out on top in a business deal and his opponent claims the method was unfair. The paranoid thrashes back, saying that if the protestor weren't so stupid he would have won but, because he was smart he took advantage of the situation, not because he was unreasonable.

These characteristics show up early in childhood; the aggressive and demanding child, the manipulative child, the sneak and the whiner. The bully is the same, and gets his way through threats and toughness.

So, how do you recognize paranoia? One way is the remarks a person makes. Here are examples that really cut into a sensitive person's inner being and are never forgotten.

A medical student was invited to the home of a classmate for Thanksgiving dinner. The mother remarked: "It's nice to meet you, but you look much too young to be a doctor." Was that necessary? Not hostile or aggressive, but just annoying and created an uncomfortable atmosphere for the student during his stay. And he never forgot it.

A young girl was recently orphaned and went to live with her aunt. At a family gathering, a woman looked at her appraisingly and remarked: "Well, when she grows up she might be a handsome woman." The child never forgot; she wanted to be pretty. Why say that to a child, especially when so vulnerable? Remarks like these are unnecessary and create damage to self-image and self-confidence.

A woman whose divorce was imminent visited her brother and his wife. She had tried for twelve years to support her marriage and had given up much in her personal life to please her husband. Her sister-in-law berated her with: "You would never give anything up for a man!" When the victim protested, she was met with a barrage of accusations and unkind words. Why? The sister-in-law's paranoid personality met resistance. The only way to get along with a paranoid is to agree with her. This illustrates the inability of the paranoid to be aware of the feelings of others. However, if a similar remark is made to the paranoid, watch out! They flare up, feel hurt, and strike back, tossing insults about. They are tremendously sensitive but have no sensitivity for others. Paranoid people are materialistic, and terribly caught up in money and possessions which seem to be their security and safety. They are in constant fear of losing these, and when they are with people—particularly relatives and friends—they are afraid they will be taken. They are not so fearful of strangers and aren't suspicious until they get to know them.

Here is an example of possessiveness. Frances Weatherby, a widow with no children, died and left her fortune to her sister, Belinda, and her two nephews and two nieces. The will instructed Belinda to divide the furnishings of her apartment and country house between them. A day was set for all to meet at the apartment and tag the furniture, but Belinda was asked to go the day before to tag hers. The next day the nieces and nephews gathered at the apartment and walked through the rooms to find every pieced tagged with Belinda's name! Then came the matter of the jewelry. The executor had given Belinda a letter from her sister instructing her to give certain pieces of jewelry to her heirs. This was a moral obligation but Belinda did nothing. The executor went twice to her house to persuade her to distribute the jewelry. At the insistence of her husband she finally did.

Belinda also inherited three grand pianos. She already had two, and a nephew offered to buy a baby grand. Belinda could not part with it, demurring: "It's in storage where it is safe, and I want to hang on to it for a little while longer." She hung on to it until she died twenty years later.

DEGREES OF PARANOIA 3

The paranoid element is ubiquitous, relating to all personality traits at will, and is constantly being turned on and off. It is never consistent.

Picture the traits of thinking and doing as two horses. When your paranoid element hops on the doing horse, you are directed into aggressive, self-seeking activities with little regard for others. When you ride the thinking horse, you are introspective, and build suspicions, fears, hostilities and manipulations in order to get your way.

So your paranoia rides both horses according to the degrees of thinking and doing you have, but not at the same time, because never, never do they come together. There is a dichotomy between them which keeps them always at odds. So there is a vast range in degrees of paranoia.

Without it you are unprotected, with it you are overly suspicious, become obsessed and are a danger to yourself and others, because instead of using it to plan ahead and play safe, it is using you. You are its instrument, driven by it to aggression if you are an aggressive person; driven to defensiveness if you are a passive person; driven to seclusiveness if you are shy and introverted. The aggressively angry person turns to destruction and is tied to high mood and assaultive, hostile and interfering behavior. He meddles in affairs that are not his concern and causes immeasurable trouble trying to control.

Most of us think things out. You hear of a house that burned down and plan what you will do if yours catches fire. Escape out the bedroom window? Or down the stairs and out the front door? You go to the city and walk the streets after dark. Should you take a siren in case you are mugged? So you plan ahead. This is normal, protective paranoia. The person who is not prepared has too little and may get into trouble because he is not concerned about what might happen and walks into the lion's den.

Some paranoids are neurotic and try to control by pressing their physical complaints on others. Their families and associates at work are plagued by their moans and groans. They are extremely sensitive to their feelings, however, so they don't really feel well, and go from one doctor to another and one emergency room to another asking for help. They are trying to control through illness.

When a doctor offers help, they find fault with the treatment, especially the medication, and claim that what is being done is wrong. This type of manipulation is typical of such a personality, and closely allied to hypochondriasis.

These people really want to feel better, but the implication when asking for help is: "Do something for me, but whatever you do is not going to help." Then they complain that the medication was wrong and the treatment made them worse, and on to another doctor. They are hypersensitive to their feelings but there is nothing wrong with their bodies. They tend to diagnose and treat themselves. Unorthodox and folk medicine especially attract them. Food and vitamin fads are also appealing with religion a close follower.

This type of paranoid person, although untrained in the skills of the medical profession, insists on making the diagnosis and prescribing the treatment, which consists of everything he has heard of. He tries home remedies, over-the-counter drugs, folk medicines, food fads, megavitamins, anything he can take or not take. He tries psychic healing, religious voodoo and the ideologies of ancient tribes. He relishes the unorthodox, which gives him a feeling of control, even though it doesn't cure his complaint. But he is right, others are wrong, and he believes he's doing the right thing in his and in the eyes of his family, who keep pleading with him to seek a doctor's advice. But he won't listen and goes his own way—never getting anywhere.

If the doctor sends him to a therapist for treatment, he objects to the exercises and offers his version of what they should be. When friends try to help, it's the same story. One says: "Try Vitamin E; it helped Sam Jones' arthritis". The paranoid returns: "Oh, no. I can't take that! I read that it is bad." Unless he conceives the idea, it's no good and rejects suggestions with animosity toward the person who offers them. But when it comes to his ideas—they are always right.

As he does not feel well most of the time, the paranoid is not a happy person. Aside from worrying about his health, he is always trying to dominate others and get them to think and do as he thinks and does and most people won't go along with this and resist his attempts at coercion. This angers him, and when he runs up against a tough customer whom he really wants to win over he may bend a bit. This, however, is extremely hard for him to do, for it is not in his nature to share. He is the king pin, he is the one who is right and everyone else is wrong. In order to get along with him you should agree with him or get into trouble.

Paranoia is inborn and varies widely from person to person. It affects people of every emotional makeup, and runs the gamut from zero to one hundred percent. It is hooked up to and influenced by other personality elements. There are thinking and doing paranoids, determined by the predominance of the thinking or doing, ranging from the extreme psychopathic (doing), like Adolf Hitler, to the extreme schizoid (thinking), like Howard Hughes. These people are withdrawn, isolated, and wound up in their feelings and thoughts; hostile, fearful, suspicious and angry. The slightest sign of assault unnerves them. When it doesn't exist, they imagine it. Usually they are brilliant—Howard Hughes, the schizoid, moral type, out to do good; Hitler the psychopathic type, amoral, controlling, manipulative and cruel.

Both types protect themselves easily, are aggressive, and suspect everyone is against them. The psychopath lumps people in a group he thinks need eliminating, and is compelled to kill—Hitler. The schizoid is afraid to touch anyone, and trusts one member only of his staff to prepare his food—Hughes.

Various degrees of paranoia extend across the population with the extremes at either end. Where is the line between enough and too much? The answer is unknown. We know that some is essential to survival, but we don't know how much is healthy or how much plays a role.

Is there an opposite to paranoia? Not really, the closest is the person with very little, and such a person is naive, gullible, trusting and innocent, fitting the adage: "Fools walk in where angels fear to tread." He doesn't suspect anyone. Comedy acts and fairy tales teach about paranoia. The skits of Abbott and Costello are examples: Abbott is a small, non-paranoid, fat man and Costello is the paranoid, suspicious, watchful, fearful. He constantly reprimands Abbott for being gullible and letting others use him.

In each fairy tale there is a trusting person who is taken advantage of. Hansel and Gretel learned that by eating the forbidden gingerbread house, they were shoved into the oven. In Little Red Riding Hood, the message is not to trust anyone—people are not always what you think they are. These fables were written to teach children that they pay in the end if they disobey. We all can learn from them.

Here is an interesting query. Is there more paranoia today? Has the human race evolved into a more paranoid species because paranoia-deficient people have not survived? Were those who lacked paranoia unable to reproduce their genetic strain because they couldn't protect themselves? These provocative questions remain unanswered, but we speculate that those who lacked have been subject to persecution, harassment, oppression and death by those with more.

What do you think of a non-paranoid person? Is he dumb? Is he foolish? Or merely childish and immature? You see him taking chances without being aware that trouble is afoot. Little children are like that. They have fear but little paranoia. Doesn't paranoia mean fear? Not entirely. There is a subtle difference, and paranoia is much, much more. The difference between the lack of paranoia and the lack of fear is that fear comes when something happens that upsets you, so you learn from that experience. Children learn some things by being taught, but they learn most things the hard way. I taught my childr to be afraid of matches. The first time I found one opening the box, I sat him down, lit a match and quickly ran a little finger through the flame. It hurt, but he never touched matches again. One son piled chairs on top of one another to reach a bureau top and came tumbling down. He learned the hard way. The paranoid doesn't have to learn the hard way. His thinking is not based on what happens to him. His fearfulness is inborn. The non-paranoid doesn't have this characteristic. He has to learn about fear.

Thus we have three levels of paranoia, high, moderate and low. Those with the greatest amount dominate the moderates and the lows. The moderate paranoids can protect themselves, grow and develop a productive and secure life, yet subject to those with the highest amount. They use their paranoia to mold their lives into more productive and acquisitive extremes, exerting pressure on the other two groups, with those at the bottom beset upon by all the others, causing an imbalance in the population. It appears that there are few with little paranoia; they are a scarce breed, which may be due to evolution.

Robert has no paranoia; he is forty and comes from a fine family. His parents saw him through years of inadequate functioning as a young person, and his teachers in grammar school said they didn't expect he would graduate from high school. He did, however, and went on to college.

Robert is naive, uncomplicated, has an easy character and is a simple, undemanding person. He has but one string to his violin. He has a sweet nature and is very passive. never challenges anybody and does whatever he is told. He is a rather limited person but has a talent for numbers and earns a respectable living as a computer operator. He works long hours and comes home, bathes the baby, does the chores his wife, Nancy, gives him. She is quite demanding and he never gets any thanks, but doesn't seem to expect any. His total passivity controls him.

Nancy's parents live nearby and are dull, overbearing, aggressive people. One day Nancy and her parents confronted Robert and accused him of not doing enough for his family. This got his back up and something snapped. He went to a psychiatrist because he didn't understand the unusual emotions he was experiencing. His tiny bit of paranoia burst out as he told the doctor: "I can't stand that!" He didn't accuse anybody but said that if they continue to do that he would leave. He said: "I'm sorry I'll leave her and the baby; I just can't stand it!" For him this was a remarkably hostile statement. He was paranoid for the first time—as paranoid as he could ever be.

The sequel is that Robert didn't have to leave. If he had he would probably have been horribly unhappy. But the family backed off when they realized they might lose their main support.

Robert leads a fairly comfortable life because he has a wife who tolerates him and work that he enjoys and is good at. Furthermore, his family is well off, very supportive and constructive, so he has many back-ups for the little world he lives in. Hopefully, his life will remain serene, for with trouble he could not survive.

Robert is the type of person evangelists attract. The lack of paranoia makes them vulnerable, so they need guidance and direction, and to be taught a philosophy that they will be saved by God or Jesus or a Supreme Being.

How does a person with little or no paranoia cope with a paranoid? That is a difficult question, for such people become entrapped like a fly in a spider's web and join the ranks of the followers rather than lead. Such was the fate of those who espoused the Reverend Jones of Guyana infamy as well as others who adhere to cults that drain them of their money and possessions and give nothing in return except a hollow faith without real meaning.

So there is a delicate balance. To keep yourself in a state of well-being, both physical and emotional—biochemical and psychological—all the systems in the body must be in balance. This can only be reached by knowing how to take care of the areas of your life, see that they are in proper balance and keep them there. This is a major undertaking and requires constant surveillance.

What are these areas? Good nutrition, the right amount of exercise and sufficient sleep. There is the expression of sexuality that is right for you, and interaction with other people that is satisfying. Others are how you handle stressful situations, distressing life events, the temptation of alcohol, smoking and drugs, and the environment with its unpredictable phenomena. All these must be dealt with.

But the most difficult area to balance is that of paranoia. Paranoia is valuable when the scale tips one way and dangerous when it tips the other. It pervades every system in the body. The quality and the quantity of the paranoia in a character is an important element in the emotional and the chemical balances in the body, because if paranoia is too low, the personality is weak, unprotected, naive, and subject to much influence from outside. If the paranoia is too high, the person is demanding, and insists on taking over even in areas of little importance in order to be in a position of control and power.

We often think paranoia is coupled with suspicion, anger and hostility, but this is not always the case. You may have too much and it won't come out as hostile control, but a desire to control for the good. So there are two faces to excessive paranoia: malignant and benign. It can control you or you can control it. Both are possible and you are the master.

The most important factors are the awareness that you have a excessive amount and how you want to use it. If your compulsion control is too strong and you don't strive to turn it around, it m become hostile. So, if you have high paranoia, use it for the good, otherwise be warned: it will control you.

But if it's too little, it's hard to add to, but this can be done if used to help someone. So, if you have a desire to control, turn it toward a good cause. You can't add to paranoia or eliminate it, but you can direct it toward necessary purposes. You can run for election or study for a profession, such as the ministry, medicine or the law. Then you will be in a position to exert influence with your desire to control and be important, and divert paranoia into channels that enhance the public good.

So where do paranoids fit in the scheme of things? Many people with excessive paranoia operate near the spillway but don't go over the dam. Those who do are the "sickies" and end up in trouble. Those who remain are vigorous, strong minded, energetic people who do much of the work of the world, turning their paranoia along the path of good. They are not particularly well liked, but they are not evil, as they use their paranoia in a benevolent fashion and the controlling aspect in an effective way that is not self-aggrandizing or dangerous.

Now let's consider paranoia in sexual performance. A paranoid man is apt to be boastful about his prowess, but is basically insecure and, although aggressive, not very effective, and may be demanding and put the blame on his partner for sexual problems. Homosexuals, males more than females, usually have high paranoia, which often is distorted by suspicion, believing they are being taken advantage of, used or blackmailed.

But don't be misled. Paranoia is important in sexuality, especially in regard to sex as a whole, not only intercourse. It's important because it melds into the love that is involved, and you control its function in order to enjoy it and please your mate, resulting in pleasure for you both.

In a compatible sexual relationship, some paranoia is good; to feel that your love is yours, that you want to dominate and control the situation and keep your mate for yourself. Without love, sex doesn't work very well. The passive person with little paranoia allows another to steal his mate. If you have no sense of ownership, that can happen. Then your love is not real, for you must be possessive for love to be valuable. This is good paranoia, intertwining itself into sexuality. Maternal and paternal nurturing is also essential, and is a part of the sexual function. You want to control your children, to mold them and teach them so they grow up responsible people. Then you'll be proud of them. This is your obsessive-compulsive need, all part of the paranoid element.

Can you imagine in your wildest dream that money and sex are similar? They are. Each person manages money and makes love in an individual way. There isn't a standard method, so no one can maintain that there is only one way. Managing money and managing love are individual and rightly so, as long as others are not hurt, so it is not fair to be critical of another's method because it is not like yours.

The paranoid quality makes you more narcissistic and involved in yourself when it comes to money and sexual expression and puts your needs above those of others. If you only have an average amount, you save your money and control it in a wise fashion. So, like a scale out of balance or a see-saw with one end up, a high paranoid quality focuses on your needs and disregards those of others, leaving you caring only for yourself. On the other side of the coin, not enough results in a benevolent generosity of careless frivolousness, often neglecting your needs. To find a balance is the goal, with the right amount of paranoia to achieve that balance, and to learn how to use it so it does not control you. In that event, a focus on the materialistic aspects of life ensues with a neglect of the emotional and intellectual.

PARANOIDS IN FAMILY AND DAILY LIFE 4

Basically, as we've discussed, paranoia is a self-protective instinct; not always destructive and hostile. You are helpless if you don't have any, and a complaining, annoying person if you have too much. Such persons have the ability to observe shades of meaning and read into them points to complain about which the rest of us put up with as a matter of course which causes disputes over petty issues. They can see through the facades people put on and point out innuendoes; they can be pompous and have a way of rationalizing that is very irritating. And where does this get them? They aggravate everyone and end up being blocked in life from achieving.

There is a plus side, however. Many artists have a good deal of paranoia in a positive sense and put into their art subtleties and refinements because of their sensitivity to the nuances in life that we don't see. This annoying/complaining element is also prominent in politicians and religious and business leaders, who point out implications and undertones unnoticed by others. Paranoids sense animosities you and I don't feel, which resolve into hostility and personal rancor, and blame society or another—never themselves.

These positive points are woven into the personalities of most great leaders and innovators of the world. In their younger years, they can see into the true essence of life with sensitivity by observing delicate shades of meaning. They can delve into the narrow crevices of understanding, examine structure as under a microscope and detect the tiny unfairnesses and flaws. An example was Ralph Nader's disclosure of certain automobiles that were unsafe, thus saving many lives.

This is the nit-picking, annoying type of paranoid. For example, the Davises and the Longs are close neighbors. Their houses are each on one-eighth of an acre and their properties abut. The driveways and shrubs are tightly aligned, and an inch or two either way could jut into the adjacent property. To most people, this makes no difference, but to the Davises it is a major encroachment into their property if the branch of a tree hangs over their line. Legally, they can cut it off, but they prefer to make an issue of it. They are extremely paranoid.

After the first confrontation, the Longs cut the branch off, but the dispute did not end there. The Davises went to great lengths to find something wrong with the property line so they could accuse the

Longs of causing it. They had surveyors over and brought their lawyer into the fray. They wouldn't speak to their neighbors and when they came face to face, gave them dirty looks. Every little thing that created friction they built from a mole hill into a mountain, and seemed to enjoy doing this. Such behavior is common in suburban settings and typical of the paranoid.

Paranoid thinking is not based on something that happens. It is based on the suspicion that it will. Fearfulness is inborn and different from fear, which you learn. When you were little your mother told you a hundred times not to touch the stove. You listened, but had to touch it once to be sure it was hot. We lived in the country, and I warned my three-year-old to play where I could see him. One day he forgot. I called and called. Finally, Spot, our English setter, nuzzled my hand and led me to little Willie, sitting on a clump of turf in a swamp, crying. He never wandered again.

Does learning the hard way stick? It seems to, especially with the person who has low paranoia. Only by experience do we learn things that impress us, and build up protection that takes care of us, but in the person with high paranoia fear and suspicion are built in. In the context of paranoia, we are the victims of our inheritance. Fear through experience is real fear with a real base. Paranoia is unreal fear with an unreal base. Fearful reaction is a normal built-in response. Paranoia is unreal, based on unreal suspicion. The non-paranoid gets along with other people; the paranoid suspects they are plotting to do him in.

Paranoids are not only men; beware the female! No one is more difficult to deal with than the female paranoid personality. She wants to control all situations and individuals in her circle of family and friends and make certain she's not hurt, but makes no bones about attacking those around her whenever she senses the slightest disagreement with her opinions. She thrives on placing someone at a disadvantage and is eloquent at putting a person down. This usually scares her victims away, and she revels in the tension she creates in order to justify her ideas, because this makes her feel she is in control of the lives around her. They appear to fear and respect her, and she can do with them as she wishes.

This woman is a past master at manipulation, and handles those close to her like puppets on strings. In this way, she can move in and throw her barbs. Tension and hostility is her life, and she constantly strikes out or defends herself or manipulates the situation for no real reason, which is clear, however, to her way of thinking.

For instance, Aunt Susan always puts her best foot forward. This fools most people because she appears to be very friendly. But beware of what is underneath; she is materialistic and fault finding, controlling, suspicious and hostile, and completely dominates Uncle George who puts up with it because he has a girl friend on the side, and his gui' makes him submit to overbearing control. Their one child, a daughter, fights viciously with her mother, who cannot understand why. Paranoids have no insight.

Paranoid personalities of both sexes are possessed with a need to be number one, to boss everybody, to have the last word and always be right. When they make trouble, which they are apt to do, they never take the blame and reject all suggestions to correct it. And they carry a grudge for life.

Are paranoids ever happy? No, for the most part. They are complainers, always criticizing. They see evil influences when they are not present and when they are they magnify them. They see intolerances, deprivations and coercions, due to their exquisite sensitivity, and oppression when it does not exist. Their suspicions are valid in some instances, and are a threat to them, posing injury and discrimination.

Leonard is a classic, excessive paranoid. He is an extremely capable man, very talented and valuable to society. He is well respected and highly successful professionally, socially and financially. However, his friends wince when he comes around because he conveys a sense of pressure which is very uncomfortable. They put up with him because of his intelligence and talent, but don't go out of their way to associate with him as he is so difficult to be with.

He is outspoken, often abrasive, and recounts his accomplishments, knowledge, and his skills ad nauseam. He claims that he is better than anyone else, tells everyone how much he knows about his profession, and downgrades areas out of his sphere of expertise.

Minorities are an anathema to Leonard. He is prejudiced against Jews, Blacks and Hispanics, and is quick to make cruel comments about them. He denounces the minority of which he is a member—an early group of emigrants to this country—and is hostile to his church. In fact, he considers that all organized institutions are out to control him, so he condemns them maliciously. So Leonard is not popular. His stream of conversation, promoting himself and putting everyone down soon becomes tiresome. Because he is a good bridge player, others like to have him along. However, one evening is usually the last. If he makes a bad play, he blames the weather, his opponent or his partner. He always has a reason for not doing well, and claims that the odds are against him. "I never get a break," his favorite phrase.

What do you do if you have to live with a paranoid? It's not easy, and the key is to agree with him unconditionally in everything he says and does, otherwise there will be constant friction. There is no middle ground, there is no flexibility or compromise. Everything is black or white. So if you have to live with one, be careful, and to keep peace allow him to control your actions and thoughts, dictate your opinions and options. It's not a happy situation.

Paranoids make strong enemies and strong friends. Those who go along with them are friends and those who don't the paranoid tries to destroy. So if you have to associate with a paranoid, allow him to be the leader and you the follower, steer as clear of him as you can, but join his camp if you have to and agree with him, for if you don't, he will turn on you viciously.

PARANOIA IN AGING AND ILLNESS 5

Paranoia increases in most people as they get older. We start out with some but all don't end up with more—we don't know why. There are no studies on this, but we suspect that the chemistry of the brain changes—probably a schizophrenic-like change—and some people are less able to fight off the resistance to the chemical derangement as they age.

In addition, we build patterns of behavior throughout life and these become ingrown, such as how to tie your shoe laces and button your shirt; brush your hair and wash your hands. And we form patterns of thinking as well. Call them habits if you will, and they remain with us unless we make an effort to change them. I remember habits of thinking I have had for years, but changing times and new knowledge forced me to change them. Many of these are formed in early years by upbringing, social and other influences. As we mature they are filtered out and abandoned or drastically altered.

Fear is bounced off by knowledge and maturity, by capacity to function and by establishing reality in life. For example, you're afraid when you're young that you won't be able to earn a living. You grow up and find you can. You're afraid you won't find a girl to marry you, you find someone who does. Your fears are unfounded, and as they evaporate through solid proof, they don't return.

It's the same with everything you take on. You're afraid you can't do it or will botch the job or won't be liked, and so forth, and before you know it, you find everything is fine, and you realize that there is nothing you can't do if you really want to. One by one your fears disappear, your self-esteem increases, contributing to a better self-image.

But the paranoid is different as he travels through life. His paranoia becomes accentuated and his fears don't vanish but increase as he ages, building up more suspicions and hostility without foundation. The more intelligent he is, the more able to invent imaginary assaults and plots against him. His whole life is molded into a network of attacks and defenses, how to think up compromises and manipulations, adjustments and controls. He has no time for just living. He is not a happy man.

It is the same with the elderly person who, in early life, may have been a bit dominating. Paranoia becomes more and more month by month, until fearful suspicion takes over and this pattern continues and slides gradually into a rut of paranoid behavior backed up by excuses. As all paranoids are good at rationalizing, this is what you get: "I wouldn't be this way if you had protected me. You should have told me not to smoke and I wouldn't have developed emphysema. I think you want me to suffer!"

The blame is always someone else's, the paranoid never admits to it, nor does he apologize. As a person ages these tendencies increase anyway, because the elderly is less able to defend himself and do the things he used to do and still wants to. As he loses control of his life, he becomes more hostile in an effort to compensate.

Paranoia is apt to blossom when there is a death in the family, especially if possessions and money are involved. Those who have a large amount of paranoia feel cheated by what they receive and claim the others got more than their share. If they are along in years they often sue. Paranoids experience a sensation like physical pain when they give up money or material things—no matter how little. Often they wind up wealthy, are greatly disliked, and wonder why.

Does everyone turn paranoid in old age? Not necessarily, but there are certain characteristics of personality that indicate a paranoid trend in a person who is sensitive, a loner, deeply engrossed in money and possessions and not particularly interested in other people. Such a person is self-involved, self-protective, but not really hostile, suspicious or controlling, and appears perfectly normal, is friendly and comfortable, but with old age and attendant illness and pain, the paranoia develops.

Here is an example. Clara was not paranoid as a young woman, but she was sensitive and interested in money and possessions. She preferred to be alone rather than with people, and seldom went out of her way to help anyone. She was a nice person, however, married and raised three fine children; her husband died a number of years ago.

Clara suffered a stroke in her eighties, and became extremely paranoid. She claims her family is stealing her money. She keeps the doors and windows locked and when her daughter enters the room she jumps up with a scream. She says the neighbors are running up long distance calls on her telephone bill—not true. When she was in the hospital, she accused a visitor to her roommate of invading her bank account and spending her money. She had never seen the man before. She is fearful of every sound and movement and lives in terror and suspicion. Her slight paranoid trend has become a florid, delusional illness.

There are paranoids in every walk of life, every profession and vocation, but those with the greatest amount are apt to choose occupations where they can influence large numbers of people, such as politics and religion, and strive sometimes ruthlessly to reach the top in order to control more. During a lifetime, paranoids go throug stages of the development of their paranoia, as through an evolution. The young paranoid is innovative, creative and challenging. He is open-minded, yet intolerant of the rigid theories of the past and seeks new ways. As he reaches middle age, he is a vehement denouncer of all theories that conflict with his, and a vigorous exponent of his opinions and ideas. His purpose is to dominate others and all situations. The methods he uses are strong and somewhat angry, although hostility, a facet of paranoia, does not show up at this stage. As he approaches the pinnacle, however, he skillfully downgrades the positions of his colleagues.

As an elderly person, the paranoid is a tyrant. He is completely intolerant of the views and beliefs of others, their feelings and judgments. He is irresponsibly selfish, greedy and miserly. He isolates himself and becomes irascible when approached. If he runs a political party or business, he is dominating and impossible to deal with; he manipulates the members of his family in a vicious, unreasonable fashion, in order to gain control of the money and the power, using any technique to accomplish this. The elderly paranoid is an extremely difficult person.

One would think that age mellows. This is not true with the paranoid, and the condition is irreversible, however, if he becomes senile, the brain ceases to function normally and the paranoid element is submerged, but if the intellect is intact, it is accentuated.

Here is the story of John Stark, a paranoid personality, as told by Peggy Downs, his companion-aide for the last six months of his life. The employment agency asked her to work for a very difficult person for eight hours daily, managing his personal needs and taking him to wherever he wants to go. His two daughters and son told her during the interview that she needed a tough skin to take care of their elderly father. This was a challenge so she took the position.

John Stark was eighty-two when Peggy went to work for him; his wife had died, and he was in and out of nursing homes. He was extremely difficult and almost cruel to his children who tried their best to please him even though his wishes were at times out of line with his physical condition.

The first morning Peggy found the patient's clothes laid out and he said: "Put my shoes on. How much are they paying you for this?" Peggy told him and he swore, stating that she was taking too long. He growled a few expletives and said: "Do you think you are worth all they pay you?"

This type of dialogue went on for the next two weeks, then Peggy gave notice. Mr. Stark looked very hostile and said: "Is that an ultimatum?" Peggy replied: "If you wish to take it that way, yes." And she flashed a big smile. He said: "God dammit, why do you look so happy?" She said: "I like feeling happy and it seems to make people around me happy too." He said: "I want to shake your hand because we will be good for one another because I am so mean and unhappy and you are just the opposite." There were no unpleasant episodes for the next four weeks.

John Stark had been a successful business man and by the time he was fifty had amassed a fortune. His father was a strict disciplinarian and not well to do, and John often went without. This instilled in him a deep-seated drive to make money, and throughout life he was dominated by greed and the urge to control. John Stark was not a friendly man and only wanted to associate with persons of wealth. He disparaged those who had little, and considered them stupid, claiming everyone has the same opportunity to make money.

As his health failed, his paranoia deepened and he became agitated and more hostile. He was irascible and stingy and criticized those who attended him for no reason, announcing that they were dumbbells and worthless if they were black or dark-skinned. He was intolerant of minorities and insulted the gentle Jamaican woman so that she cried and left the job. He had attendants around the clock but Peggy was the only one he related to. She was kind, understanding and had the patience of Job, and after a while he seemed to be totally under her spell. He held back his foul language at her insistence, but was rude, impolite and swore at all the others. His thoughts were concentrated on his money and possessions: "Where is my checkbook? Where are my cars? Has my son put the money in the bank?"

Once John Stark insisted on going on a cruise to Alaska. This required two companion-aides, Peggy and a young male attendant. The trip was for them a nightmare. John Stark shouted at the dinner table that the food was no good—why couldn't they learn how to cook properly? He criticized everybody and everything. He was afraid to be left alone and if Peggy spoke to another person he yelled that she was neglecting him.

Peggy quickly learned how to take a situation out of John Stark's control by saying: "O.K., if you won't be a gentleman, we are going right back where you live and I will tell your family. Then I will give my notice." Stark behaved properly for a while, and came to respect Peggy and admitted that he loved her. This surprised and shocked her, for she had no designs on the elderly man or his money and wanted no part of what that admission might foretell. His attachment to her was not lost on John's children who immediately conjured up the specter of a change in beneficiaries to his will. Suffice it to say that Peggy was the only person who could handle their father, so they put their fears aside until one day, John Stark fell and became partially paralyzed, incontinent and bedridden. Peggy put up with her "challenge" until she could no longer be useful—she was a companion, not a nurse. John Stark died a month after Peggy left.

THE PARANOID PERSONALITY 6

So what do we mean by "paranoid personality"? Does it mean insanity? No. Does the person have delusions and hallucinations? No. It simply means that a person is compelled to control other people and all situations he becomes involved in. How does he go about satisfying this need? He begins with his family, but this small group does not suffice, so he chooses a vocation that commands large numbers of people. The most obvious are the political, financial and religious routes, so he plans ahead and prepares carefully. To be a politician, you should enter the law, to rise in the financial world, you should be well versed in economics; if religion is chosen, divinity or rabbinical school is indicated. These are not the only fields in which one can dominate and control, but most paranoid personalities seem to end up in them, for if they are successful and rise to the top, they become visible for all to see. They like that, for the paranoid personality is also obsessed with power and influence, and revels in hoarding money and possessions. They are aggressive, materialistic people.

All extreme paranoids show evidence of these traits early in life, and it's important to understand that they are born with them. They are not acquired because of poverty or early trauma or parental influence. They are genetic and cannot be changed, and are there to stay from birth. Therapy cannot eliminate or soften them, nor can a normal home life of love and affection. The environment—no matter how strong the impact—has no effect.

Another common facet of paranoia is an overpowering amount of energy, much more than the average person has. Paranoids are driven by an inner desire to prove themselves right, to be the big shot, to be the boss. They have a tremendous drive to exert influence, emanating from a limitless need. The paranoid person is filled with fear. This is closely related to the drive to control, in reality it's the fear of not having control. This element is not a delusion or an hallucination—it is a paranoid fear. Call it an illusion or a misinterpretation, if you will, and it is neurotic in the extreme.

This fear drives the paranoid to protect himself from others whom he has no reason to fear, as well as those he does, so he tries to find a safe position where he can be comfortable and out of danger. But he never finds such security. He is frightened all his life, and as he grows older, having hurt many people, fear worsens. He doesn't give a whit about those he has injured, he only cares about how he can be secure and comfortable.

All the attributes of being excessively paranoid, the hostility, the fear, the tireless drive to control, the suspicion, the egoism, the criticism, combine to make a driven, intolerant, hostile, aggressive, self-serving, egotistical, unpleasant person. Experience tells us that a paranoid personality does not come full bloom from a happy, comfortable family. As a rule, there are paranoid elements in the parents that show up in the child in minor ways, coming to full fruition in later years, usually in the forties or fifties.

As you read on, you will find that some extreme paranoid individuals begin their careers inspiring others and doing good deeds. They are revolutionaries, challenging existing authority and vowing to make the world a better place. Their intentions appear to be motivated in helping people; their speeches are uplifting, promising a better life for all. The secret agenda of all paranoids is to establish control and, as their stories unfold, they gradually change as they drive into middle life. Spurred on by high energy and perseverance, they have achieved their long sought power and the opposition is cowed or liquidated. Then they seek every means to perpetuate control for their own ends, totally oblivious of the needs of others.

Whenever awareness is triggered that their control is being eroded or challenged, paranoids react violently. They cannot share it, nor can they listen to another's ideas; they can only hear their own. They become dictators, tyrants and slave drivers, feeling only their needs and unable to appreciate the suffering of others, which they observe with dispassion. They consider themselves benefactors to mankind and press on, conscious solely of their own gains.

Getting control demands innovative and constructive thinking which calls for high intelligence and energy. Once achieved, it requires dominating and persecutory paranoia. As paranoids strive for control they are innovators and when they finally arrive they are persecutors. Thus, the quality of paranoia changes but the goals are always the same: control and the elimination of competition, with ultimate total power and domination.

Today, we are experiencing a huge increase in unnecessary murders, robberies, and assaultive actions. You hear of men robbing the cash register in the corner store, taking the money which never amounts to very much, then killing the storekeeper. Usually, the answer is drugs, because paranoid qualities are enormously enhanced by the use of drugs, particularly crack, the most prevalent use of cocaine. Cocaine sparks the paranoid reaction, which in turn creates the impression that you are in danger and will be killed for robbing the store, so the self-defense mechanism is inflamed into aggression, the excessive paranoia takes hold, and the scenario results in the "fight flight" syndrome, resulting in murder to assuage the paranoid fear.

Just as personality types are unique—no two alike—so it is with the paranoid personality. There are a variety of types; call the extremes "malignant" and "benign." Hitler and Stalin are malignant; Churchill and Howard Hughes benign. There is the aggressive paranoid and the passive paranoid; the bright and the dumb paranoid; the forceful and the weak; the high energy and the lazy paranoid. And each is linked to his or her other inherited personality traits. The aggressive/extraverted paranoid is active, and spends his energy controlling others; the passive/introverted paranoid is busy defending himself. Thus the self-protective element is exercised in the individual's own fashion. Paranoids have symptoms that verge on the psychotic, but they are not psychotic; their emotional systems work as though they were out of control, but are actually planned and directed toward their goals in a most shrewd and unemotional manner.

Here are examples of paranoid personalties in everyday life. Melissa is married and has two boys and two girls. She is a poor mother and seems incapable of warmth and caring. Her entire drive is for personal success and power. She tries to control her husband and children, but spends little time with them, preferring to be out of the house spreading her influence about the community. When she's at home, she is most unpleasant, finds fault with everybody and bawls out the children for the most minor infraction.

Melissa is a joiner. She joins civic societies, religious groups, social groups and political organizations, and works her way up to chairman or a position of importance. She wants to be head honcho, then she has power and control. She gives freely of her time and energy and achieves considerable success. She has become almost indispensable to the community as she is always willing to head up another action committee or run the garden show or organize a fund raising effort for the church. The community depends upon her because of her influence in practically every movement. She is also active socially, hauling her long-suffering husband to this function and that benefit; no wonder she has no time for her family.

Melissa always projects a good image, gracious, sweet and smiling, exuding friendliness. However, this vanishes once in contact with her. Then one senses a feeling of repulsion, which is typical of the paranoid, who promises everything and gives nothing. She is singleminded, selfish and caught up in being bossy, abrasive and controlling. She has to be at the top of the heap in all situations. She loves to tell people what to do, so she is always available to set up banquets and parties and organize outings. In this she works very effectively, and ould have done the same for her family, but has no time or interest for ersonal life.

The paranoid always causes disruption, and Melissa is charting a course that can only end in personal failure and the disintegration of her family. Her husband is divorcing her and has left with the children, who are completely alienated from their mother. Now she is alone and unencumbered by family responsibilities, is she happy? Or even content? Probably not. Paranoids are hyper-sensitive and take everything as an insult or a plot against them. They are right and the world is wrong. Melissa blames the breakup of her family on her husband and the children.

Norman was born and died an impossible paranoid personality. His father was a difficult, controlling man, and there was a history of emotional difficulties and several suicides in his family. Norman was a bright, capable man, but also very controlling, caustic and difficult. He drove his family to distraction with demands and counter-demands, and manipulated them to such a degree that one son suicided.

In a fit of anger and depression, he attempted suicide himself, but failed, sustaining a severe, crippling disability from which he never recovered. He used this for more manipulations, coupled with an absurd suspicion that his family was about to hurt him and take his money. His hostility was vicious. He had wild ideas that those who took care of him were plotting to kill him and he rejected the medications upon which his life depended, manipulating himself into dying from neglect of his health.

Just before his death, his anger was so fierce that he rewrote his will, cut his wife and children out and left his entire estate to a mistress whom he had not seen for seven years. His retribution was beyond comprehension, but was his way of getting back at his family. And for what?

Sharon came from a relatively poor family and married Raymond, a well-educated man with an upper class background. His father is the top executive of a large corporation and his mother a socialite. The young wife has alienated herself from her parents-in-law, and keeps her husband from them on the grounds that they are out to get her. She writes long letters explaining that the attitude of the parents is so poor she can have nothing to do with them, and asks for money without compunction. She blames the father for trying to force her to do things against her will, and protests: "Who is he to tell me what to do, just because he's a big shot!" She is hostile, manipulative and unreasonable, rigid in her opinions and cannot be budged. She is a typical paranoid personality.

How should the parents handle this? Go along with her and agree with everything she says and does? Yes, because if they oppose her they will lose all chances of seeing their son and grandchildren. If the marriage lasts, they must praise her and stress her good points, never mentioning her bad ones.

The individuals whose careers are outlined in the following chapters are thinkers or doers with extreme paranoia. Their personalities can be interpreted by how they act through life, that is, if they show sensitivity, empathy and consideration for others or a lack of these qualities. In every case, note that the paranoid element dominated their lives, resulting in a distortion of character, with a focusing on selfish and intolerant attitudes.

These are dominant and vital people, however, whose influence has been enormous, some beneficial and some destructive, but never insignificant.

It is our opinion that the paranoid element introduces a dynamic force into the structure of personality; a force that may result in good or in evil. Whatever degrees thereof, the paranoid quality will produce an overpowering influence, predominantly evidenced by control and self-directed goals. Suspicion, hostility and anger are the qualities we usually expect in a paranoid person, but control and self-aggrandizement are the qualities that are more basic. From these may spread innovative and constructive growth or restrictive, greedy and unrepentant ruthlessness.

And how can you tell which course paranoia will take if it can go in either direction? It depends on how the person uses this force, partly due to his basic personality—whether more thinking or more doing— and partly on how that individual's environment affects him during his formative years. However, no matter which course it takes— toward good or toward evil—it is a controlling, dominating, greedy and unrelenting force. Such a person also has extremely high energy, and the combination produces high mood, approaching euphoria. He never stops, but becomes caught up in the strength of the drive, much as the tumbleweed being blown across the plains by a windstorm, on and on, never coming to a standstill.

These people are not "sick," not mentally ill like the paranoid schizophrenic who thinks the Communists are coming in the front door, or fears that people are talking about him, and who hears voices telling him to buy a gun and shoot the president. They are mentally normal, but are endowed with innate characteristics of energetic paranoia.

In contrast, the low energy person with high paranoia is another breed entirely, and could not perform like the person with high energy. The paranoia of these people drifts down into nastiness—gossipy women, bitter old men, petty bureaucrats, throwing their weight around at low levels so as to make themselves appear to be big shots, trying to be important at others' expense. So this type of paranoid also invades our lives, forcing upon us their unreasonableness, jealousy, picky, fault-finding natures.

And where does crime come in? Is it linked to high paranoia? Yes, low energy coupled with low intelligence produces a strong tendency to criminality as shown in the petty thief and other low-level law breakers. Such people are easily caught but rarely learn from their mistakes and are often career criminals.

PARANOID COMMUNITIES AND NATIONS

7

THE ONEIDA COMMUNITY

Not only are people paranoid, but a community can be also, as illustrated in the story of the Oneida Community, a benign dictatorship, which came into being due to the efforts of one individual—John Humphrey Noyes . He created a utopian society. Though small—never more than three hundred souls—its members considered it to be the ideal environment in which to live, love and die.

John Noyes graduated from Dartmouth with a law degree, then studied religion at Yale; he was ordained a Congregational minister in 1833. A rebellious young man, he formed his own doctrine of right and wrong, and a year after his ordination announced from the pulpit: "He that committeth sin is of the devil!" This provoked criticism: "Noyes is crazy, he says he is perfect!" Soon he was notified that his license to preach was revoked and he must leave the seminary. But John Noyes clung to his concepts of what was right, even though stripped of his church, his family, and many of his friends. For the next few years he wandered about, preaching his faith to whomever would listen—often hungry, often penniless. During this time he solidified his position on marriage, sexual intercourse and the family, to whit: "...in a holy community, there is no more reason why sexual intercourse should be restrained by law, than eating and drinking, and there is little occasion for shame in either case."

In 1838, he returned to his home in Putney, Vermont and married Harriet Holton. He was reunited with his family, taught Bible classes and published THE WITNESS. In 1840, he established the Putney Association, the principal objective of which was to spread the gospel of salvation from sin, to preach Christ and act out the spirit of the gospel as a family. He enlisted as members a group of religious persons who agreed to consider themselves one family.

In 1844, the Association adopted communism—today called communal living. This included the theory of Complex Marriage and Male Continence, literally birth control. This was too much for Vermonters, Noyes was indicted for adultery, and advised to leave the state. He moved the "family" to the Oneida Reserve in upstate New York and in 1848 formed the Oneida Community consisting of eighty-seven persons, fifty-eight over fifteen and twenty-nine under. The adults were of varied professions and trades and were sufficient to maintain the needs of the group. During the first year, they built the Mansion House, completing it before the onset of winter. Everyone worked together, including the women.

Then John Noyes and his senior advisors decided how they would live, what their duties should be and how to share the details of daily living. One of the houses was assigned for children from two to twelve, with housekeepers and teachers to care for them; another was a nursery for the infants and their nurses and housekeepers. Most of these duties rotated. Meals were served in the Mansion House. Everyone received the same food.

During that first year, the women had difficulty working in their long, full dresses, and several leaders cut them into short frocks and made pantaloons to wear underneath. All the women soon followed suit. Then, to save time and energy for more productive use their long hair was cut.

The members gathered every evening for roll call and to give them a chance to air ideas, suggestions and grievances. Each evening was devoted to a different subject: current events, music, dancing, lectures and readings. On Sunday there were lessons from the Bible, followed by discussion. Next, "mutual criticism" was introduced in order to improve character. Every person came under the scrutiny of four judges appointed by the Association, who gave their opinion of the moral character of the individual. This was intended to motivate the person to correct his shortcomings.

Thus, the Oneida Community grew and prospered, and attracted small colonies from New York and surrounding states to join them. In 1851, a Connecticut couple donated their farm of 200 acres, and members formed a colony there with a school, a silk thread factory and a spoon factory. Back in Oneida, they had a printing office, which published THE CIRCULAR, and a sawmill, a machine shop, a flouring mill and a carpentry shop.

In 1864, the community's net earnings were $155,000.00 and 1880 a half million dollars. The chief industries were steel traps, sewing silk, preserved fruits and vegetables. The tableware business, which continues to this day, was started in 1877.

There were no marriages among the members of the community. The concept of Complex Marriage was that each person was married to everyone else. This was initiated in order to limit the number of babies for economic reasons and to avoid pregnancies except those planned between specific mates. Therefore the practice of Male Continence, birth control, was begun. John Noyes chose certain older men whom he considered to be of the most upright character, intelligence and experience, to initiate into the practice of Male Continence. This initiation is not explained but it was the rule laid down by Noyes that young persons should associate sexually only with older men and women.

John Noyes felt from the beginning that to be sinless one must share one's possessions with everyone. He was thirty-five when he decided to introduce his philosophy on sexuality into the group, and the opportunity came when his wife, Harriet, received a love letter from Charles George, a married man and his associate. Harriet showed John the letter confessing that she reciprocated Charles' sentiments.

Apparently, this episode precipitated Mrs. George's confession that she was in love with Mr. Noyes and willingly gave her husband to Harriet. Then John Noyes professed to love her. The four in this cross-union considered their love was from God and the manifestation of unselfishness, while selfishness meant keeping a mate exclusively to oneself. Noyes felt, however, that the four should postpone the consummation of their desires in order to give him time to prepare his flock for Complex Marriage and remove the community out from under the cloud of sexual notoriety. He surmised that some of his followers would not accept this display of adultery.

Noyes' rationale was that God was at last ready for Complex Marriage, whereby all the men would be husbands to all the women. He ordained that contacts would be made on the "social plane", and the only prohibition was that propagation would be controlled by him. He would decide which couples were scientifically suitable to have children in order to produce a superior race. Thus the practice of Perfection would be achieved.

Harriet Noyes had four stillbirths before their only son, Theodore, was born, and the terrible suffering she experienced caused John Noyes great grief. He tried celibacy, but that didn't work out so he began experimenting with "male continence," which he defined as the art of prolonging the act of intercourse as long as possible without exposing his mate to the risk of pregnancy. This was at the expense of his own climactic pleasure, which under the Noyes system was to be avoided, i.e., a man should not be deprived of the pleasure of orgasm. Noyes claimed that he so perfected this art that Mrs. Noyes experienced "great satisfaction." Furthermore, his system made possible sexual freedom and satisfaction of all members of the commune without interfering with the scientific production of children or "stirpiculture," as it was called.

John Noyes preached that the "union of men and women with God was the most important and union with each other the second, and that the two were so intertwined that neither could be fully achieved without the other". He recognized the "natural timidity of women," but monogamy offered but "scanty and monotonous fare." He said that intercourse of the sexes was a form of worship when done under Noyesian auspices. If a woman was reluctant or hostile to his philosophy, he usually won her over by stressing that the act of physical love was the sign of inward grace—of "the resurrection". If someone loved husband or wife but would not share that person with another, he or she was not worthy of a place in the Kingdom.

Thus, Noyes gathered into the fold men and women and couples to enrich the population and resources of the Oneida Community, which soon numbered 200. Why did people join his movement? Because he approached them as an evangelist saying he would help them strive for Perfection and when they achieved it they could join the holy group of Perfectionism. Were they attracted by sex or religion? The answer is that Noyes coupled the two as one, so all were satisfied, and he turned away those who regarded Perfectionism as merely sex or only religion. He claimed that those at Oneida were the only people who truly possessed the foundation stone of Christianity--the selflessness of sharing mates.

How were the arrangements made for these "special visits" in order to share? Although the adults all lived in one large house, it would not have been proper for a man or woman to walk about searching for the apple of his or her eye, so the overtures were made through a third person, preferably an older woman. This was considered an ideal way, for if the person approached was not attracted to the suitor, he or she could gracefully refuse without causing embarrassment. No doubt this custom was breached more than once, and ardent couples took matters into their own hands, as all were free to visit in one another's rooms.

Usually the advances came from the woman, so it was considered quite proper for a lady to approach a man which she usually did with an unmistakable glance, a wink or a gesture of coquetry. Thus, the gentleman, if not intrigued, could gracefully bow out by ignoring the look or pretending not to have understood. During the time of scientific breeding, however, this manner of courtship was superfluous because John Noyes insisted on choosing the couples who were to produce babies. One can easily imagine how greatly the public was piqued by curiosity about the amatory customs of the Oneida Community!

Anxious apologists for Noyes are wont to declare there was more to Perfection than sex. There was also more to the Mississippi than the palace steamers, but it was those craft that brought the world rushing to the bank to goggle. And it was the amatory customs of Oneida which interested the public. This is not strange, since it was the central point of interest of these `Bible Communists' themselves, coloring their entire existences, as one remarked, with a `rosy glow,' even for individuals whose powers had cooled." Life for all adults excepting the few celibates who were permitted to remain, was a serie of overlapping courtships, each with the hope of fulfillment. Too, in the children's quarters marriage fodder was sprouting higher by the year to brighten one's maturer existence." (Escape to Utopia)

Consequently, Noyes taught the young people according to his own lights and that there is "nothing wrong or unclean about their sexual organs, and nothing sinful in their sexual desires." Furthermore, they were taught that to fall in love would bring nothing but disappointment. The girls were instructed that to lose one's maidenhead was of utmost importance and that a mature man should give her this experience before being free to choose men of her own age, who might be apt to abuse the privilege.

It is a matter of record that John Noyes fathered the majority of the children in the breeding experiment and therefore felt he was the one best qualified to sacrifice himself in elevating the young ladies to a spiritual plane during this one moment in their lives. At the same time, the boys were initiated into this spiritual experience by women past the menopause. The reason the young people should not make love with one another, i.e., on "the horizontal plane" or with those younger—"the descending plane"—was that this would not bring a "spiritual link and chain" of ascending fellowship to "connect the experience with God." To fall in love or to hold a "special love" for someone was the worst of Oneidan sins.

Noyes' system of birth control theoretically prevented the loss of seminal fluid, and when he decided that the Community was prosperous enough to allow the bearing of children, it was conjectured that the men may have become infertile because of this, which later proved to be untrue. Many of the women, however, had passed childbearing age, so Noyes decreed that the men could father one child provided the woman each chose was acceptable to him, and only superior parents could have more than one child.

A group of young men and women petitioned Noyes to permit them to have a child or to pair them up as he deemed fit, and most of the women hoped he would choose them for himself, which he undoubtedly did. Although he was sixty and failing in health, he managed to father nine "stirps," as these experimental babies were called. There were of course "accidents"—babies conceived by young people in love who had taken matters into their own hands. However, these were few, as most obeyed Noyes' orders.

Since the inception of the Community, Noyes had planned to provide for the expense of children when they were able to afford it. That time came in 1869, and he and his advisors created what they called "Stirpiculture," known today as eugenics, whereby a committee chooses the individuals considered best suited to bear children. Eighty young people were chosen and by 1879 sixty-two babies had been born, but there it stopped due to the incipient break-up of the Community.

In the second and third generations of the membership, factions arose to dispute the structure of the Oneida Community, caused by the loss of strong leadership by Noyes, whose health was failing, and he moved to Niagara Falls in 1879 to escape the barrage of criticism and threatened litigation regarding what his critics called "free love." And the young people challenged the practice of Complex Marriage; they wanted to live together as husband and wife and have natural selection of a mate. The thinking began to change as young people were sent to college and learned the ways of the real world, became sophisticated and some agnostic. This led to the desire to fall in love and be married as others were and many questioned the teachings of John Noyes. Furthermore, they objected to his autocratic rule and wanted more freedom in Complex Marriage and a say in the management of the businesses, for even though he had moved away, his people remained loyal, and he still exerted leadership, although this had weakened.

At John Noyes' request, his son, Theodore, although an unbeliever of what his father had created, took over as leader and brought with him a young woman, Ann Hobart, to work with him. However, severe criticism soon arose about management policies and Ann was forced to resign, ending Theodore's reign. The Community limped along for a year or two under the absentee leadership of John Noyes and his loyal supporters, until an onslaught of criticism was thrown by the local clergy. The bishops and ministers of the Diocese of Central New York, threatened to "blot out" the Oneida Community as an "insupportable spot of immorality on the escutcheon of fair New York State." Although this group had never approved, it had for the most part left the Community alone, but this effort created a deep and serious wound.

In addition, signs of greed and tendencies to control showed up in the actions of the men who ran the businesses, which had always been under communal ownership. Although John Noyes wrote a directive, he was unable to stop the trend. Then came pressure from the "generation gap" of the first group of young people who went to Yale and Columbia, which increased with each class of students. The age of science had arrived and was applied to religion, obviating the doctrines of John Noyes who, to give him credit, studied Darwin, Mendel and Galton, but never changed his original belief in God and Jesus Christ. The Oneida Community, however, was in its decline.

Who was this extraordinary man, Noyes? He believed deeply that what he was doing was right in the eyes of God, and adhered strictly to the teachings of Christ and the Bible. He established methods by which his people worked to better themselves, physically, spiritu ally and mentally. He strove to help them improve their disposition their relationships with others, their consideration and love of the fellow man. He was highly intelligent, intuitively wise and of a warm nature, and had inherited the gift of leadership. He radiated security, and imbued inspiration into his followers. He held that Complex Marriage is completely justified by religious percepts, and explains his dogma of sexuality in detail with excerpts from the Bible.

John Humphrey Noyes may well be called a "benign dictator." What he conceived, attempted and to a large extent carried out successfully, was a utopian life for up to three hundred persons living happily, in good health, and leading active, productive lives. This went on for more than thirty years and ended when his health began to fail and the only controlled experiment in selective breeding of human beings came to an end.

Noyes was a benign, paranoid personality of great magnitude, with the highest motives, who, as we've said, believed in God, the Bible and the teachings of Christ. His only faults were his inability to change and his overpowering paranoia which compelled him to control the thoughts, actions and deeds of his followers. When challenged, he was adamant. He was rigid in his concepts of what is right; and, although he studied the changes that were taking place, was unable and/or unwilling to accept them. He was greatly attached to his son, Theodore, but rejected his and all ideas of a younger generation. He died in 1886.

The dissolution of the Oneida Community came in 1881, and the businesses were absorbed into the communities in which they were located. One remains in Oneida—Oneida Limited, Silversmiths.

Although never documented, the Oneida Community is the only controlled experiment in human genetics on record. It is the opposite of what is practiced by all animal species and most of the human race, i.e., natural selection of a mate.

SPARTA

Not only are communities and people paranoid, a nation can be also, as illustrated in the following vignette on Sparta and in the chapter on Adolf Hitler, whose paranoia increased as he lost control of the war to such an extent that national paranoia ensued.

In the eleventh century B.C., one of the four great branches of the Greek nation were the Dorians, who derived their name, according to legend, from Dorus, the son of Helen, and subsequently built the four Dorian towns from which sprang Sparta.

Sparta conquered the surrounding towns and villages, and by the fifth century B.C., controlled the entire lower section of the Peloponnesus. At this point, the citizenry was divided into three groups: the Spartans from Dorian descent, the helots, or serfs, who were forced to do the menial work and grow the crops, and the Perioeci, who concerned themselves with commerce and manufacturing.

The Dorian descendants were the ruling class and occupied themselves with the chase and war, with an emphasis on controlling the peoples they had conquered, which they did by becoming a warrior society. Seven-year old boys were removed from their families to be educated by the state and trained for war. They grew up in barracks, learning discipline and austerity, and became the best warriors in Greece. The word "Spartan" is today a by-word for endurance, rugged frugality and self-denial.

By this time, Sparta and Athens were the two ruling powers in Greece and under constant friction. The interaction between them was vicious. The Spartan philosophy was paranoid: singleminded, warlike, dominating, aggressive, hostile and suspicious. The background of the Athenians was Ionian, whereas the Spartans was Dorian—and the words Ionic and Doric are used today in architecture—the strong, unadorned Doric columns and the slender, elegant Ionian. The Dorians were in many ways the reverse of the Ionians, retaining the antique style, solid and grave, and at the same time hard and rough. The word Doric is used today to describe the Scottish dialect—broad and rough in contrast to the Ionic—delicate and smooth—English. In addition, Spartan women wore the tucked-up hunting dress, while the Ionian men wore long graceful garments.

While the whole of Greece evolved into a paranoid nation, the Spartans during their heyday surpassed the Athenians. This was apparent in their culture: to be hostile, to conquer, to subjugate, to be arrogant, controlling and always right.

In the fifth century, Sparta suffered setbacks, including a revolt of the helots and Perioeci and the Third Messenian War. However, Sparta prevailed in the Peloponnesian War which ended with the conquest of Athens and the leadership of all Greece.

Finally, in the third century B.C., Sparta suffered defeat by Phillip II of Macedonia and the Achaean League, and in the second century joined the League. This was destroyed by the Romans in 146 B.C.

What is learned by this? We learn that too much paranoia can make and then break a nation, can make and then break an individual. Sparta is ancient history. In modern history there are many examples of nations and individuals who have dominated and gone on to destruction, carrying with them the death and excruciating suffering of millions, mentally and physically. The subjugation and control of millions of people who yearn for freedom goes on today.

PARANOIDS IN BUSINESS

8

JOHN PIERPONT MORGAN

John Pierpont Morgan was born April 17, 1837 in Hartford, Connecticut to Junius Spencer and Juliet Pierpont Morgan. He was a sickly child, and his health prevented him from attending school for any length of time. By high school age, however, his health had improved and he went as a boarder to Cheshire Academy.

At a young age, Pierpont demonstrated signs of high paranoia. He was self-willed and, when crossed, sulked. He was quick to criticize and even questioned the answers to arithmetic problems in the primer. Overall, he was a bright student. In the meantime, his parents moved to Boston, where he spent his last year in high school and subsequently graduated second in his class. Throughout his schooling, he showed a strong propensity for mathematics, and was a good athlete and excelled in every sport he undertook.

At that time, Junius Morgan became a partner in the London banking firm of Peabody and Company and moved his family abroad. The Morgans were accepted into the social whirlwind of London and entertained and were entertained lavishly. They enjoyed the company of the highest society and were presented at court to Queen Victoria.

Pierpont was sent to school in Geneva to prepare for the university, where he perfected his French and learned German, but his greatest talent was for mathematics. Junius decided Pierpont should attend the Royal University of Gottingen in order to receive the best background in international finance. He was accepted there by his classmates who were mostly of proud birth. They loved to carouse and sing songs around the piano in the beer cellars, in which Pierpont always joined in his loud bullfrog voice. He had a large capacity for drink and smoked a pipe which he changed to cigars at an early age. He learned to fence and became a fairly good swordsman. He also took riding lessons and hacked around the campus for exercise.

Pierpont was a handsome young man with dark hair and eyes, full-lipped and always carefully groomed. He had inherited a prominent nose from his grandfather John Pierpont, and all his life was plagued by eczema, which produced a redness on his nose which lasted for weeks, and embarrassed him immensely. He cut a grand figure, however, with his powerful physique and height, always clothed in the most stylish and expensive manner.

When Pierpont was twenty he graduated from the university and was offered an apprenticeship without pay in New York with Duncan, Sherman & Company. He had an allowance from his father and lived as a paying guest with the Dabneys. His social life was full. He was invited for weekends out of town and for dinner by friends and business associates of his father. He was entertained by Morris Ketchum, his father's former employer, and was introduced to the Sturges family with whom he became acquainted at St. George's Episcopal Church on Stuyvesant Square which they all attended. He was particularly attracted to Amelia, called Mimi, a petite, attractive brunette two years his senior. In the meantime, he toiled at the office, working at cost accounting and bookkeeping, which he thoroughly enjoyed. He was an avid and fast learner, and had a quick grasp of figures.

Then the panic struck. The end of the Crimean war suddenly cut the demand for American wheat, impoverishing the farmers. Many small banks which had loaned speculatively went under, resulting in the failure of hundreds of factories and businesses. The railroads suffered as well and the stock market followed. Pierpont made a decision—he must earn a living and be on his own. He asked for a modest salary and was promoted to junior cashier. He curtailed his social life and studied late into the night—banking, currency and shipping. He retained, however, his association with Mimi to whom he was becoming more attached, but couldn't think of marriage until he was well on his way toward making money.

Junius suggested that Pierpont learn the cotton business, so he went to the New Orleans office to learn the trade. There, he got involved in a cargo of Brazilian coffee which he paid for with Duncan Sherman money, and cleared several thousand dollars for the firm and was awarded a generous commission. Elated by his success, Pierpont decided it was time to go into business for himself, and rented a small office at 54 Exchange Place, where he quickly built up a clientele of customers for whom he traded securities on the exchange.

Abraham Lincoln was elected president and the Civil War began. Pierpont, pleading uncertain health, avoided the draft. However, it is true that he suffered frequent headaches and bouts of eczema. During the war, his business flourished, but Pierpont was despondent because of Mimi's failing health; she had developed a cough which was diagnosed as tuberculosis. They were married in October 1861 and she died four months later. Pierpont was devastated. At twenty-four, he was a sorrowing widower, and visited her grave every year for the rest of his life, such was his devotion. He remained in deep mourning for a full year, eschewing all social affairs and devoting himself to his work and church going.

The following year Pierpont emerged from his chrysalis of sorrow and once more relaxed with friends. He worked all hours at the office, however, and his business thrived as the war gave him the opportunity to dabble in gold bullion, in which he made a killing. However, the bull market in gold finally subsided and Junius persuaded him to join with Charles Dabney. The firm of Dabney, Morgan and Company came into being in 1863.

Although Pierpont Morgan had a powerful sexual appetite, undoubtedly his marriage to Mimi was not consummated, and it is presumed he was still a virgin when he married Fanny Tracy in March 1865. This was no love match, but for Pierpont it afforded him dividends in comfort without personal inconvenience, but he would never become reconciled to the loss of his only true love, Mimi. Fanny Tracy was a practical, sensible girl willing to play the role of wife and mother, and to run his household. The first of their three daughters, Louisa, was born the following year and a son in 1867.

Pierpont had always shown a penchant for leadership, organizing weekend picnics in his youth and dinner parties and gatherings as he grew older, when his paranoid tendencies began to be unmistakable. In his work he was meticulous and highly critical of inefficiency. He had an autocratic manner, but all agreed that the functions he organized were well managed. These abilities placed him on committees and boards of directors on which he relentlessly forced his colleagues to accept his suggestions.

He had to control, but it must be said that his management technique was successful, although his modus operandi was not always the most acceptable. He exerted the same style at home and dictated his wife's choice of clothes, their color and cut and the way she did her hair. They soon were entertaining lavishly, and he planned the menus, and placed the guests at the table. He had a house on Madison Avenue and a summer place at Irvington-on-Hudson, from where he commuted daily by train to his office. He hobnobbed with the rich and famous, both those whose characters were shady and those who made their fortunes honestly.

At this time, Pierpont was about thirty years old. He had grown a mustache and the rosy condition of his nose, diagnosed as acne rosacea, became more accentuated as he grew older. He was very reserved and seldom came out of his shell. He ate and smoked to excess which aggravated the acne and his health, and he suffered from insomnia and dyspepsia.

Pierpont was a prejudiced man, prejudiced toward the Jews who were taking over part of the social and business scene, and intolerant of all who were not born into the class of social standing and breeding which he enjoyed. He joined the elitist Union Club where he spent much of his time when away from the office. His health and temper suffered when Abraham Kuhn and Solomon Loeb gained access to the Stock Exchange, and was deeply resentful when President Grant named Joseph Seligman his financial advisor. This precipitated a severe case of acne rosacea.

A vacation was ordered by his physician and he and Fanny went to California by train and stagecoach. Along the way he discovered that a John D. Rockefeller had taken control of the oil wells in Ohio, and founded the Standard Oil Company of Ohio. In the interim, Jay Gould and Commodore Vanderbilt had gained control of the Erie and New York Central Railroads, and Pierpont was spurred to action when he heard they were out to take over the Albany and Susquehanna. He moved in fast, bought enough shares of stock to gain voting power at the annual meeting and was voted in as vice-president, thus gaining control for himself and his associates. Gould was soundly defeated by Pierpont's brilliant maneuver.

Then ensued a battle royal for the railroads between the "good guys" and the "bad guys." Gould, Fisk, Boss Tweed of Tammany Hall and Commodore Vanderbilt on one side; Pierpont Morgan, Andrew Carnegie, John D. Rockefeller and Chauncey Depew on the other. Then Gould sparked off a bull market in gold ending in Black Friday, September 24, 1869, in which many fortunes were lost. The "good guys" won this round, but it was not the end.

Pierpont was thirty-three and Fanny in her third pregnancy when Anthony Drexel of the Philadelphia banking house asked to join him in a liaison between the Drexel and Morgan banks, and with Junius Morgan's London firm, they created an international banking house. They had built a huge edifice of white marble on the corner of Broad and Wall Streets in Manhattan, costing one million dollars, with elevators, among the first in New York. It was 1871 and it still stands today.

The prejudices of John Pierpont Morgan stood out like sore thumbs. They were evident in the manner in which he dressed, high wing collar, flowing cravat, starched cuffs and heavy gold watch chain. His cold, hard stare intimidated most who came within his pervue, showing his snobbishness for all not included in his upper middle-class, well-bred, Episcopalian background. He had little respect for entrepreneurs such as Will Durant, Bernard Baruch and E.H. Harriman—later events caused him to change his mind.

Pierpont's paranoia was apparent in many ways. He liked to run things and demonstrate his magnanimity. He smoked huge black cigars and was seldom without one between his teeth. He was an avid church-goer and fancied himself a model Christian. He ruled his office and his household with an iron hand. He acquired a summer place called Cragston in Highland Falls across the Hudson river in New Jersey and had his yacht ferry him across from New York. He continued to entertain extensively, but when the whim seized him, which it often did, retired to a spot away from his guests and left their entertainment to Fanny.

Although only in his mid-thirties, Pierpont's health was not of the best, due to his lifestyle. He was grossly overweight, his blood pressure was high, and his exercise consisted of walking from his office to his carriage and in and out of his house. His smoking exacerbated his acne, which flared up often, so his nose looked like a huge strawberry. His disposition deteriorated when this happened but his spirits revived when he took a trip abroad. Expense was no object, and he traveled with his family from country to country, exhibiting enormous energy, leaving Fanny exhausted.

Although he maintained that his marriage was happy, Pierpont began to spend less time with his family and dined often with men friends at the Union Club or Delmonico's, where there were private supper clubs frequented by business associates accompanied by "widows" and their coquettish "nieces" and "cousins." They were stylishly dressed and lived in small houses in the best districts. Pierpont, of insatiable sexual appetite, adjusted to this double life with gusto.

By this time Pierpont was more involved in ocean liners and commercial shipping than the railroad industry, which was in trouble, but a significant turning point in Morgan history took place at this juncture. William Vanderbilt, son of the Commodore, William Henry and Chauncey Depew offered Pierpont the opportunity to buy 250,000 shares of the New York Central Railroad. The Commodore had died and left his fortune to his son, Billy, who was shy, insecure and a devoted family man who never smoked or drank and was totally unfit to manage his father's vast empire. It was recommended that he sell his shares of New York Central to the Morgan bank, which he did.

When hearing of this, Jay Gould decided to take over the railroad industry and cut Drexel, Morgan out. However, he didn't succeed, as the Morgan officers were on the watch for such a move, as well as for other interesting opportunities, such as the Edison Electric Light Company, which they underwrote in 1878 in order to finance the incandescent light bulb, Thomas Edison's invention. The story of its success is history.

Fanny and Pierpont built a huge mansion on Madison Avenue and 36th Street, the first to be fitted throughout with Edison's incandescent lighting, powered by a generator dynamo in the stable. At this point, their church, St. George's Episcopal, was in need of a Rector, and a young Irishman, Dr. William S. Rainsford, was appointed. He gave controversial sermons and was enormously popular. Dr. Rainsford was probably the only individual Pierpont ever gave in to during his long life. They had a disagreement, and it was the first time Pierpont couldn't get his way with the wave of a check. It almost broke up their friendship. However, Rainsford persisted at reconciliation and Pierpont finally conceded because of his need for spiritual support.

Pierpont preferred a structured life, adhering to a rigid schedule and seldom varied the time he arose and went to bed, arrived at the office and left. He was a compulsive committee member, attending all meetings of boards of directors, stockholders and charitable and religious organizations. His contributions to the proceedings were brusque and brief.

Pierpont was generous with his fortune, but kept a tight rein on his extensive holdings in railroads, telegraphy and Edison franchises. He worked very hard, often burning the midnight oil and was at all times au courant with every detail of his holdings. He salvaged many a worthy project that was about to fall by the wayside by underwriting the deficit.

At this time, E. H. Harriman was managing the Illinois Central which Pierpont had ignored as being insignificant, but he became interested and bought two-thirds of the stock, placing him on the board of directors, a meeting of which was held in Pierpont's library, attended by the principals of all the railroads. After considerable opposition, Morgan exerted his personality and finally succeeded in establishing a coalition through which prices and policies could be stabilized. The meeting ended in a gentleman's agreement which led to the term "Morganization." This established Pierpont Morgan as the champion of investment power, which had an impact on the Congress, labor leaders and industrialists. In the ensuing years, Pierpont Morgan tried to dominate all who opposed him, at times his paranoia taking precedence over his better judgment.

In 1880, Junius Morgan died in an accident and Pierpont took control of J.S. Morgan and Company in London as senior partner. He became acquainted with the Rothschilds, the famous and powerful Jewish bankers, and regardless of his prejudice, became captivated with Alfred de Rothschild, especially enjoying his good taste and superb collection of art works. While in London, Pierpont entered into several lucrative business deals with the powerful financial institutions of Baring Brothers, the Rothschilds and others. He was sure of their credit and didn't hesitate to offer his two banks, J.S. Morgan and Drexel, Morgan, to further the deals.

Back in the United States, Pierpont resumed his life of affluence, entertaining and womanizing, and continued to wheel and deal in the financial world. One of his maneuvers was the merger of the Edison General Electric Company with its greatest competitor, toppling Henry Villard from the presidency and removing the name of the inventor from its title. It emerged as The General Electric Company.

The more success Pierpont experienced, the more his autocratic nature augmented, and his paranoia was increasingly satisfied as he exerted control over this company and that individual. Although feared by many, he usually worked toward the good—for the country, for those he deemed worthy and, of course, to further his career and holdings. Thus, he became a formidable figure in the financial worlds of Europe and the United States. With all his power, affluence and prestige, essentially he was a good man and a religious one.

Pierpont was also a generous man. He contributed to the establishment of many charitable and religious organizations: the Cathedral of St. John the Divine, the Lying-In Hospital, the Union Club, the Metropolitan Club, the Metropolitan Art Museum, the New York Yacht Club, the Morgan Library, to name a few. He contributed enormous sums of money to the Episcopal church and to charity, and when hearing of the misfortune of some individual, forwarded funds to clear up the debts. Morgan's philanthropy was impulsive, sentimental and limited almost exclusively to those with a personal claim to his regard. For instance, he did not support those of the lower classes or the strikers rioting for decent working hours.

Pierpont liked to plan, organize and manage. He insisted on executing to every detail a wedding in the family. He was reserved, sensitive and proud, but never got over the dreadful disfigurement of his nose, however, he always encouraged the companionship of beautiful women with whom he liked to be seen.

Pierpont Morgan's affinity for power was evident in an incident at the Union Club. One of his nominees for membership was blackballed by the Committee, and Morgan retaliated by starting a new club, the Metropolitan Club on the corner of Fifth Avenue and Sixtieth street. He didn't resign from the Union Club but boycotted it with his friends for many months. When he regarded the Committee sufficiently punished, he returned.

Further evidence of Morgan's paranoia cropped up when his son, Jack, became engaged to Jane (Jessie) Grew, but was disgruntled when her parents insisted that the wedding take place in Boston. Pierpont had offered to stage the entire performance but was politely turned down. He had his day, however, when his daughter, Juliet, married William Hamilton a few years later. He planned and managed the entire scenario, from the floral arrangements, the menus and the gowns of the bride, her mother and the bridesmaids. None outwitted John Pierpont Morgan in his flamboyant display of wealth and good deeds. He had to be the biggest and greatest.

His taste, however, was subdued in the marrying off of his four children into solid New England's "haute bourgeoisie," and he watched with pleasure the disastrous results of the marriages of his peers' children who wedded into Burke's peerage or a titled European family. He disdained their penchant for buying Europe's blue blood with American greenbacks.

On the surface, the marriage of Pierpont and Fanny appeared happy, although Fanny must have been aware of Pierpont's infidelities which, however discreetly handled, were common knowledge. Throughout his entire career, he never ceased his womanizing, which may have contributed to his intense dislike of publicity. He was especially enraged at the rumor that he agreed to sponsor the Lying-In Hospital, which his doctor for a long time had been anxious to build, because one of his mistresses had been delivered of his baby by the good doctor!

In 1893, a recession gripped the country and the stock market was deeply depressed. Railroad shares took a beating and the Union pacific was in trouble from years of mismanagement and corruption. Morgan was called in and headed a committee to keep the line running and backed it with gold notes. The other railroads were also faring badly, and Morgan reorganized the Northern Pacific and rescued the bankrupt Erie Line. The recession worsened; stocks slumped and unemployment soared.

As time went on and Morgan closed one successful deal after another, his arrogance increased and his paranoia fed into grouchiness whenever he was challenged. He was quick to criticize the work of others, became angered when he was found fault with, and withdrew his support if he detected the slightest impropriety in management.

Pierpont Morgan had an affinity for tall, handsome athletic young men. There was never a hint of homosexuality—his pursuit of the opposite sex disproved this but this inclination highlighted his disappointment in his own appearance, his nose and that he had allowed his body to deteriorate into an obese, flabby, mass of flesh, due to the excesses in which he indulged. Enter young Robert Bacon, the scion of a family with a pedigree, a graduate of Harvard, Pierpont's preferred college. He dressed well and his manners were impeccable, his physical attributes were outweighed by his qualifications in ability and intelligence. Morgan offered him a junior partnership which he accepted with alacrity. Bacon was the epitome of Pierpont's ideal of an Adonis, and soon became his right hand man—almost a second son.

Shortly before Pierpont retained Robert Bacon, Anthony Drexel died. Thus, he became head of the two international banking houses, with total control, and changed the name to J. P. Morgan & Company in London and New York. It was 1894 and Grover Cleveland returned to the White House. Morgan, who regarded all politicians as self-important fools, or rogues who sold their principles to the highest bidder, was disturbed by the administration's handling of the gold issue. Gold bullion was being shipped out of the country until a paltry nine million in gold coin remained in the vaults of the Treasury. This was shaking the confidence of Wall Street.

Pierpont and August Belmont went to President Cleveland who refused to receive them, but was finally persuaded by his secretary of the Treasury that the country must be saved from insolvency. He accepted their offer to form a syndicate of sixty-one members of the financial community to float an issue of sixty-five million dollars in gold bonds. These were heavily subscribed and Morgan again saved the day.

During the next two years he worked out a merger with James J. Hill, a powerful magnate in the northwest, between the Great Northern and the shaky Northern Pacific railroads. His success was criticized by William Jennings Bryan, the fiery demagogue from Nebraska, who opted for a silver standard over a gold. Morgan was besieged by slander spread by Bryan's silver lobby, claiming that the president was a tool of Wall Street and Morgan was making millions under the table. Cleveland's term was drawing to a close, and Morgan joined with Mark Hanna, chairman of the Republican National Committee, to choose a candidate to run against William Jennings Bryan. They picked William McKinley who won easily.

It was 1897, and Pierpont was now enchanted with the Adirondacks where he spent a vacation, and bought a one thousand acre estate there. Then, he bought property adjacent to his house on Thirty-Sixth Street, and had built a larger library to house his vast collection of first editions, manuscripts memorabilia, priceless tapestries and carpets. His yacht "Corsair" was commandeered by the Navy during the Spanish-American war, so he had built the "Corsair II," one hundred feet longer, with a crew of sixty-nine. He took delight in the New York Yacht Club and was jubilant when the "Columbia" defeated Sir Thomas Lipton's "Shamrock" for the America's Cup. In addition, Morgan had the mansion on Madison Avenue, the estate, Cragston, the London residence and Dover House in Roehampton. Then he added a fishing box at Newport and an apartment at the Jekyll Island Club in Georgia.

Morgan's sojourns with attractive women did not moderate. He continued his pursuit of courtesans, and consorted with men of money and position who also enjoyed the orgies to which he was addicted. He was sixty-two and regularly patronized two ladies in Bar Harbour and at Aix-les-Bains in France, where he had taken a fancy to a French-woman and rented a chateau for her. At home, he frequented Delmonico's and held parties with his friends who also were inclined to collect numerous paramours.

One wonders at the attraction beautiful women had for this aging, flabby body of two hundred and twenty pounds, ugly of face, a bright red nose, his eyes the only redeeming feature. The comfortable love nests, the expensive jewelry, the charge accounts must have been the appeal, for Pierpont never ceased to captivate them. Scandalmongers attempted to unearth evidence of his amours, but none could ever be found—only the fact of his womanizing, which was widely known. Such was his discretion in these matters.

Among his favorite public figures was Lillian Russell, on whom he called regularly "to advise on her valuable collection of Chinese porcelain," although it was known that she was the companion of "Diamond Jim" Brady. He was introduced to the actress, Maxine Elliott, was dazzled by her beauty, and continued to see her for many years. She acquired a series of lovers along the way, all common knowledge, but her affair with Pierpont was conducted in great secrecy. This was ever his way.

Enter John W. Gates, a vulgar and flamboyant gambler, who started as a hardware clerk and somehow made enough money to form the American Steel and Wire Company. He asked J. P. Morgan and Company to finance a holding company, so Morgan put together the Federal Steel Company in three months, gathering Illinois Steel into the fold, the only competition, which had merged with the Minnesota Iron Company. Morgan was now deeply into steel. However, Andrew Carnegie's Pittsburgh Steel overshadowed the thriving Federal Steel, so Morgan decided to create a combine, organized and financed by 23 Wall Street, in order to dominate the world market. This policy worked with the railroads so it should work with steel.

While the good guys and the bad guys were trying to swallow one another up, Morgan left for Europe to add to his rare collections of ornaments, paintings and jewels and plan his daughter, Louisa's wedding. She was to marry Herbert L. Satterlee, a match he highly approved of. They wanted a simple wedding but Pierpont insisted on a lavish ceremony at his Madison Avenue house, and had constructed a huge marquee and a dance floor that would accommodate two thousand four hundred guests. He supervised every detail, the floral decorations, Louisa's entire trousseau and the gowns the bridal party wore. On his return, he engaged an architect to design his marble library and amused himself poring over blueprints and materials. It would cost several million dollars.

One by one, the steel men, Schwab, Gates, Carnegie and others each tried to control the industry, but Morgan was too much for them. He bought out Andrew Carnegie, then Gates, and with his Federal Steel, in 1901 the United States Steel Corporation was born. It had 168,000 workers and controlled over sixty percent of the nation's iron and steel output, plus miles of railroads. Charlie Schwab was made president and Judge Gary chairman, with Bacon, Steele, the two Rockefellers, Henry Rogers and Peter Widener on the board of directors. Excluded were Gates and Harriman because of Morgan's dislike for them. The public rushed to buy "Big Steel" and within seven months a million and a half shares were sold.

Charlie Schwab was in his prime at thirty-seven, and enjoyed his presidency in a manner that was difficult for Judge Gary to stomach. He squandered money on expensive limousines and pleasure, touring Europe, consorting with the Rothschilds and other high-living dignitaries, and gambling, surrounded by coquettes. Pierpont admonished him for his self-indulgence, however, they parted amicably, Schwab professing to mend his ways. Even though obligated to censure his behavior, Pierpont realized he was much too valuable to dismiss, for he was running United States Steel Corporation with outstanding skill, and the company was prospering.

J. P. Morgan & Company was no longer a private bank, it was selling stocks and bonds directly to the public. Because of publicity about the steel trust, Pierpont was pestered by reporters, and often offended by articles, and cartoons that always accentuated his nose.

His many successes caused Morgan's paranoia to blossom and he contrived to control his enemies and their holdings, namely, E. H. Harriman, the Rockefellers and Jacob Schiff. His plan was to set up a new holding company—the Northern Securities Corporation to acquire the stock of the Northern Pacific and Great Northern systems and form a transportation complex between the Great Lakes and the Pacific. He then invited Harriman and Schiff to join with him and include their Union Pacific holdings. The Northern Securities Corporation was launched in November in New Jersey, but Harriman declined to contribute his Northern Pacific holdings.

At this point, President McKinley was assassinated, and Theodore Roosevelt became president. Morgan agreed with Mark Hanna, who proclaimed that a "wild man" and a "damned cowboy" was now President of the United States. One of Roosevelt's first acts was to determine what role the Government played toward large corporations. Should it control them or not? At that time, there were no laws or regulations. He chose the Northern Securities for the courts to determine whether it was a monopoly and an illegal restraint of trade. This was a challenge to Pierpont, whose power was unique; he had saved the nation during the gold crisis, amalgamated the steel industry and restored order to the railroads. There is no doubt that he would he equally successful in dominating the world's shipping lines.

Knowing this, Pierpont was filled with euphoria which led to egomania, resulting in a self-image of invincibility, free from criticism and moral, legal and political censure. His paranoia puffed him up— he could do no wrong. He had the "unconscious arrogance of conscious power." Then President Roosevelt struck. His Attorney General announced a suit to dissolve Northern Securities Corporation under the Sherman Anti-trust Act. Resentful but seemingly unmoved, Pierpont left on his annual trip abroad, leaving his cohorts to complete the mergers and acquisitions he had engineered in the rail, steel and shipping industries.

In January, 1901, Queen Victoria died and Edward VII took the throne. Pierpont had met the king through the Rothschilds, and he was very cordial to Pierpont during that interval and they found much in common. The London social season was in full swing awaiting the coronation, to which Morgan and his daughter, Anne, and son, Jack had been invited. However, the mad whirl of frivolity did not deter Pierpont from adding to his possessions of paintings, sculptures and other objets d'art and last but not least to busy himself putting together the steamship lines, the White Star, and the Leyland and Dominion. The Cunard, the largest, was less receptive, but the Hamburg-American Line was interested in joining the cartel, and Pierpont went off to Germany to meet with Kaiser Wilhelm and personally woo it.

But Morgan, in his arrogance, experienced a stunning defeat. He had not reckoned with the pride of Britain and Germany, and the hostility engendered by an upstart country flying its flags over its ships incensed the two imperialistic countries, already suspicious of each other's naval power. So negotiations with the International Mercantile Marine ceased, and the Morgan firm was stuck with $150 million worth of unsold securities. It was evident to all except J. P. Morgan— and he would never admit it—that the failure of this enterprise was due to him alone. His partners, Steele, Perkins, Baker and Widener shared in the defeat and the responsibility of its disastrous history. All lost money.

In 1903, Pierpont lost the anti-trust suit against Northern Securities and appealed to the Supreme Court. The stock market was shaken as confidence in railroad shares decreased, money tightened and companies went into bankruptcy. U.S. Steel slipped and the fiasco of International Mercantile Marine cast dark shadows on Morgan's integrity as his enemies chortled, but Morgan retained his self-confidence that the court would rule in his favor.

With all this mud flying about, the columnists and cartoonists had a field day. Pierpont received his share with his friends. Enter a con man and blackmailer, "Colonel" Mann, who put out a scandal sheet called TOWN TOPICS, filled with anecdotes of the "rich and famous," their antics, orgies, and adulteries. The information came from "below stairs," valets, maids and chauffeurs, who were handsomely compensated. To stay out of TOWN TOPICS, Morgan, Schwab, Huntington, Thomas Fortune Ryan and many others paid Mann "loans," the sum of which amounted to a large fortune by the time he died in 1920.

Charlie Schwab, not having forgotten the rebuke by Morgan, resigned the presidency of U. S. Steel and, through clever manipulations, took back Bethlehem Steel. He formed a new corporation which became one of the world's largest steel producers, second only to

Morgan's combine.

Morgan was convinced that Theodore Roosevelt was out to throttle big business and went to great lengths to find a candidate to run against him during the next election. He found few who were interested. Little had been done in the anti-trust area since Northern Securities, which the Supreme Court declared "an illegal combination or conspiracy in restraint of trade," and the onslaught on big business appeared to be subsiding. Roosevelt won a landslide victory in 1904, and Pierpont met with him on common ground when his company was appointed fiscal agent for the transfer of $50 million to Panama for the purchase of the French Panama Company's stock which would go toward building the Panama Canal.

Robert Bacon was forced to resign because of broken health from overwork, and Pierpont brought his son Jack and his family from London to fill his place. He built a house for them on the corner of 37th Street and Madison Avenue, then busied himself with plans for the Triennial Convention of the Episcopal Church which the Archbishop of Canterbury would attend. The Convention and the attendant festivities were all arranged by Pierpont, including a visit to Washington where he introduced the Archbishop to President Roosevelt.

J. Pierpont Morgan wore blinders when it came to anything outside his realm of birth, upbringing and education. His milieu was conservative New England, his education class-ridden Europe, so he was out of touch with changing social trends and the growth and aspirations of his country. His environment was the office, in which the "dollar" reigned, his various houses, "Corsair III," the Episcopal Conventions and his nineteen exclusive clubs—a narrow scope, indeed. He traveled in a manner which none other enjoyed, and with all the attention money could muster. He never had the slightest concept of what it was to be poor, or hungry or unable to buy the necessities of life.

Morgan's eminence in the banking field and his superb collection of art works earned him a cherished accolade—the presidency of the Metropolitan Museum of Art, which he held until he died. He donated many treasures to the museum and enrolled as trustees his wealthy friends who, with him, made good the annual deficit. He ruled with an iron hand, appointing those in positions of power whom he considered the best fitted for the job, regardless of objections.

True to the progression of paranoia with aging, Pierpont, now sixty-eight, became increasingly self-assured, irascible, demanding, critical and obsessed with power to the point of total insensitivity. He was intolerant of the opinions of others, and this spilled over into his stewardship of the museum. It was difficult to work with him—it had to be for him.

Having been successful in anti-trust endeavors, the Roosevelt

administration turned to the insurance companies. Roosevelt created
the Legislative Investigating Committee with Charles Evans Hughes
as chief counsel and the Equitable, Mutual and New York Life Insurance Companies came under attack. It was claimed that they had used
their funds to finance the promotions of Standard Oil, Harriman, J.P.
Morgan and Company and Kuhn Loeb. Morgan & Company suffered
the least, and Harriman was the main scapegoat, attacked by the press,
the Democrats and the church.

Pierpont was now absorbed in the final completion of his library,
and transferred to it thousands of books and artifacts which were in
storage and in his various abodes.

During the winter of 1906-7, he suffered from several colds and
his rosacea flared up so badly he curtailed his social activities, and took
a trip to Europe, collecting more art objects and paintings. On his
return, the news from Wall Street was ominous, but not disquieting
enough for Morgan to cancel his trip to the Episcopal Triennial
Convention in Richmond. Coincidentally, President Roosevelt went
bear hunting in Louisiana, which helped to stem the rumors of pending
chaos in the economy.

During the panic of 1907, Morgan virtually kept the Stock Exchange open and saved New York City from bankruptcy. Never had
his remarkable leadership been more apparent. Returning from the
Convention, he met with the presidents of the banks and private
financial interests and through his masterful capability for organization called an emergency meeting, roped in his opponent bankers and
the small bank presidents and placed the dire circumstances before
them. He knew who could contribute their share, and threatened and
coerced until they finally agreed to chip in all they could, pledging the
hundreds of millions of dollars needed to bail out the banks. Then he
approached President Roosevelt for the government's share, which
was forthcoming. However, the reprieve was short lived, for the real
need was for gold bullion which was frozen in London. Pierpont
cabled Jack, who shipped three million dollars in gold. The day was
saved, with Morgan again at the helm.

Pierpont spent the next few months rescuing this bank and
saving that corporation, wheeling and dealing, but always for the good
of the nation. Finally the tension broke, the market steadied, and Wall
Street relaxed; but the result was a depressed economy, which money
could not correct. Unemployment soared, wages shrank, crime increased.

One might think that J. P. Morgan, at three score years and ten,
had earned retirement to travel and enjoy his art works, but no, he
preferred to solidify his position over and over as the undisputed
paragon of American finance. Many openly disliked him, but respected him and grudgingly admired his ability. Nor did his age lessen

his appetite for beautiful women, although his romance with Maxine Elliott began to fade because of her many trips playing to admiring audiences. It is rumored that he was the leading light in her success in the stock market.

The 1907 crisis brought several of Morgan's competitors into a closer alliance—the Rockefellers, Stillman, Harriman, Gould and Thomas Fortune Ryan. He managed to maneuver directorships for several of his henchmen onto their boards of directors and took pleasure carving up Harriman's empire. He continued to perform good works; he added to the Wadsworth Atheneum, founded a Yale Chair in Assyriology, and endowed the Harvard Medical School, which won him an honorary LL.D. And true to his concern for his fellow man, when Harriman lay dying, he went to his bedside and made up with him, parting as friends. Harriman died a few days later.

Actually, Morgan was less interested in Harriman's holdings in the railroads as he was in the Guaranty Trust and Equitable Life. Two of Morgan's partners went on the board of directors of the Guaranty and soon the two companies were absorbing weaker companies in banking and insurance. Nothing seemed to check Morgan's mastery to acquire wealth as he forged interlocking voting directorships among successful banks, three trusts and the leading insurance companies, including 50,000 miles of railroads, the United States Steel, General Electric, International Harvester and the American Telephone Company.

At the turn of the century, the automobile appeared. By 1908, Henry Ford had introduced his Model T "for the average man." William Durant, an insurance salesman, was close behind. He had salvaged the decrepit Buick Company in 1905 and soon outsold the Model T. As "the average man" could not afford an automobile, both companies ran into financial difficulties. First Durant, then Ford, approached J. P. Morgan & Company for funding, but both requests were turned down. However, Will Durant struggled along, formed the General Motors Company and added the Oakland and the Cadillac to his line of Buicks.

It was here that Pierpont made a mistake in appraising the potentials of a company. He appeared more interested in the archaeological findings in Egypt. His interest in Egyptology was kindled by Alfred de Rothschild, who introduced him to Lord Kitchener and General Sirdar of the Egyptian Army and the Count and Countess of Carnarvon. He cruised with Thomas Cook, with whom he studied the history of the region, and became fascinated with the lives of the Pharaohs and their kingdom.

Pierpont's judgment failed him again when he refused to lend money to Bernard Baruch to investigate a sulphur dome in Texas. Baruch received the loan from the Guggenheims and they all made a killing. Perhaps it was racial bias on Morgan's part, but a short time later this was offset by quixotic generosity to Henry Duveen, also a Jew, who had undervalued a shipment of art treasures and needed one and a half million dollars to pay the duty.

John Pierpont Morgan was clearly assuming the role of the elder statesman, focusing more on the exhibits at the Museum and foreign travel than trekking to 23 Wall Street. He was seventy-three and concerned himself with business issues of no less than five million dollars, major policy decisions and senior staff appointments, and he personally handled matters of policy that involved the White House or the government. He seldom visited his clubs, but always attended the Episcopal Church Conventions and meetings of the Metropolitan Museum of Art. Contrary to the classic progress of the paranoid personality, J. Pierpont Morgan appeared to be mellowing in his old age.

During 1911, Pierpont was involved in plans for the construction of the Titanic, which would make its maiden voyage the following year, when he was given notice that President Taft had brought suit against U. S. Steel on the basis that it was a monopoly. Woodrow Wilson was nominated by the Democratic Party to run against Taft and subsequently won. It was the beginning of a new era for big business.

On his 75th birthday, Pierpont received the news of the sinking of the Titanic. This came as a shattering blow not only for the loss of life, but to the competition, the Cunard Line. Pierpont turned for solace to travel and treasure hunting regardless of expense, and had shipped back the largest collection of all time. It filled three hundred and fifty-one huge crates, and all went to the museum.

On his return home, Morgan learned that he had to appear before a Senatorial Committee investigating large contributions to presidential campaigns. This annoyed him, for he had nothing to hide and was infuriated at the insinuations and the inconvenience. He emerged unscathed, however, but annoyed by implications in the press of influence peddling. J. P. Morgan was not in good humor. These happenings irritated and depressed him and he was particularly annoyed when the board of trustees of the Museum dragged their heels about providing a wing to house this last collection of treasures. They argued that Morgan could well afford to provide the funds himself as he had done for the Lying-In Hospital and the Maxine Elliott Theater. Pierpont became more and more grumpy, and the election of Woodrow Wilson added to it. Nothing seemed to be going his way.

Pierpont intimated that he may not bequeath his collection to the Museum, and by the time the City Fathers allocated the funds, he had arranged to have it removed to his library.

Now the Congress sprang into action and investigations began into events leading up to the 1907 crisis. A Committee was to deter-

mine whether a "community of interest" developed between 23 Wall
Street and the country's banks, trusts and insurance concerns. This
was direct attack on Morgan's personal integrity and his firm's policy!
Harriman and Standard Oil's Rogers were dead, Stillman and
Rockefeller were sick men, so it was left to Morgan to appear at the
hearings.

Samuel Untermeyer, a relentless prosecutor of big business and
champion of organized labor and his fellow Jews, was chief counsel for
the Committee, and unexpectedly proved to be a fair interrogator. The
press, however, was vitriolic and antagonistic. Morgan arrived in
Washington with a retinue of eight lawyers, and stalked into the
committee room filled with spectators and photographers. He testified
for two days, answering questions without reference to notes. He
seldom lost his poise, but at times had to go on the defensive, and was
irritated by the innuendos that what he did was for power and lust for
money. He said sharply: "If it is good business for the interests of the
country to do it, I do it."

Pierpont was badly shaken by this experience and left for Europe
on his doctor's advice. Before, however, plans were drawn up to create
the Federal Reserve Act, drafted, ironically, by a team headed by Paul
Warburg of Kuhn, Loeb, the firm that had so often opposed Morgan.
He revised his will, leaving his art collections to his son, and sailed
with his daughter Louisa. Pierpont was not himself; he slept badly, ate
little and did not enjoy life. Past events had taken their toll. Doctors
could find nothing to cause his depression and physical complaints.
Louisa, alarmed, cabled for his doctor to come from the States with
Herbert Satterlee. Pierpont perked up at their arrival but again became
disconsolate at newspaper versions of the Committee's report, one
excerpt of which stated: "The acts of this inner group (Morgan-Baker-
Stillman) have been more destructive of competition than anything
accomplished by the trusts, for they strike at the very vitals of potential
competition in every industry under their protection..."

Pierpont organized a trip to the Pyramids but found it difficult to
walk. A specialist found his blood pressure high, and suggested a
change of scene. They went to Rome and settled into a suite in the
Grand Hotel. On Easter Sunday, Pierpont attended church with the
Satterlees. A few days later, he suffered a stroke, and lost his speech,
fell into a coma and died in his sleep March 31, 1913. He was seventy-
five.

The day of the funeral, the New York Stock Exchange closed
declaring: "In the development of our country, he contributed more
than any man in our day...The whole world has lost a wise counselor
and a helpful friend." Theodore Roosevelt declared that "any kind of
meanness and smallness was wholly alien to his nature." Samuel
Untermeyer said: "A man of rare breadth and public usefulness...who

was animated by high purpose and never knowingly abused his almost incredible power." Pulitzer's newspaper, often critical of Morgan's business philosophy, proclaimed: "No man clothed with irresponsible, autocratic power could be expected to wield it more honorably or ably or patriotically than he."

John Pierpont Morgan was a great man. He did more than any person of his time to mold this country into the great nation that it is. He had an extreme paranoid personality and a benevolent schizoid (thinking) nature, evident in his reserved manner, his proclivity for work and solitude, his sensitivity in matters of human relationships, and his altruistic bent. If he had been psychopathic (doing) he might have been a Hitler or a Stalin, but to him the good of the nation was of paramount concern. His thinking side was dominant as illustrated in his idealistic, creative, sensitive, and philosophic personality with focus on things—his precious art works—rather than people. If he had been more doing than thinking, the manipulative, sneaky side would have been dominant, dealing more with people than things, and the greedy, self-satisfying, cruel, suspicious side of his nature would have been more prominent. In both types, however, the strong, controlling drive is always evident—one for good the other often for evil—both for power.

Yet, Pierpont displayed a dichotomy, in that parts of his personality were in direct conflict with others. He was very religious, yet a philanderer; he was idealistic, and moralistic, yet exploited his strong sex drive without remorse or conflict.

JOHN H. PATTERSON

John H. Patterson was born in 1844 to a large Ohio farm family, earned a degree at Dartmouth College and went into business. He married at forty-three, and became a widower six years later when his wife died of typhoid fever. She left two children, to whom he paid little attention.

His first job was peddling coal for a local company, at which he did well but lost his job and went into business with his brother, Frank. They bought interests in coal mines, a railroad and opened a miner's supply store. Much to his surprise he lost money, but soon discovered the reason—his clerks were dipping into the till. In those days, cash received was kept in an open drawer, receipts were not given nor was the money tallied daily. While searching for a solution, Patterson happened upon a machine which turned out to be the first cash register. He made $5,000 profit in the next six months.

In 1883, the company which held the patents to the cash register issued stock and the Patterson brothers bought all of it, gaining control. John's benign paranoid tendencies began to emerge—he had to have it all. They renamed the company The National Cash Register which it remains today. Their factory turned out thirty machines a month but apparently there was no market. Patterson cast about for a method to promote his register and came up with the idea of deluging prospective customers with promotional mail. For three weeks he sent six pieces to each person on the list, praising the virtues of the cash register. This was the first business venture into direct mail as a sales technique.

In those days, and to some extent this holds true today, the salesman was the typical drummer, the glad-hander, who in a sense was selling himself, and had a certain personality that portrayed this image. They did not sell a product but claimed they could sell anything—themselves. Patterson decried this technique and changed all that, replacing the backslapping, glad-hander with a well-trained, well-mannered sales representative—selling cash registers.

Through trial and error, he set up guidelines for his salesmen. His plan was to mold them to an image he could control. First, he established territories with penalties for encroaching on another's ground—always the paranoid influence. Then he demanded that his salesmen look and act like gentlemen in dignity, dress and manners. He taught constraint in speech and behavior, and that the "customer is always right." Then he called on his most successful sales representative to develop a sales talk, which turned out to be the first "canned" approach to sales.

He had printed a selling primer, and set up training seminars which all had to attend. As an example, the answer to the statement by the prospect that "I can't spare the money," is "Which money? All we ask you to spare is the money you are losing now." Answers to similar sales-resisting questions were in the primer and the salesmen developed others.

In 1892, there was a precipitous drop in scrap metal prices. The notion that this foretells a severe business depression was popularized by a midwestern farmer and regarded by some as gospel. Patterson adhered to it and it turned out that he was right. The Panic of 1892 broke six hundred banks and 15,000 businesses failed, but National Cash Register enjoyed record sales. His methods were proved. In subsequent years, sales continued to climb, regardless of the four-year depression that followed, and in 1910, 100,000 cash registers were sold, and the next year the millionth mark was reached.

But all was not easy going for Patterson. The depression invoked discontent among the labor forces of many companies and created resentment, sabotage and, for some, arson. John's greatest blow was a $50,000. shipment of cash registers to England which were defective—

someone had poured acid into the machines. Patterson went to the root of the matter and discovered that his employees had little enthusiasm for their jobs and no reason to put out good work. He delved further and became aware of the deplorable working conditions his employees were subjected to. The workplace was dark, dirty and uncomfortable, the wages were low and there was little if any chance for recognition or advancement.

As was his way, Patterson vigorously proceeded to correct matters. He gave a general wage increase, cleaned up the workplace, installed dressing rooms and showers and a cafeteria. He introduced safety measures to protect his workers and provided a dispensary and free medical care. He rebuilt the factories so that daylight filtered through the glass sidings. He had the landscape developed into lawns and gardens and attractive walks with shrubs and trees.

The workers too, maintained Patterson, required "something to stimulate ambition". To start, he instituted a plan to pay for suggestions—the first time in industry. Then he attempted to give his employees a thirst for knowledge by providing a night school where they learned the techniques of their work, general knowledge and what was going on in the world. All this was free and included lectures and concerts.

John Patterson was highly criticized for these endeavors—a waste of time and money, exercising "paternalism." But he wanted his programs copied by others so he opened his factory to the public, and gave tours and lectures on his programs. Some claimed this was welfare, but he denied it was charity, that it increased productivity, reduced poor work and generated ambition and contentment in his workers. He issued a house organ, the NCR Weekly, which was eagerly read and enhanced acceptance of the mandated training for sales, factory work or any position with NCR. Only his executives escaped his regimentation. By the turn of the century, John Patterson had achieved what he had been striving for from the beginning of his business career—the control of his operations through training, education and the building of an allegiance to him and his company by the employees. In a sense, he was a benign dictator of his small domain, and once under his control, he was assured of a secure footing and could go on from there to unleash his driving urge to do whatever his impulsiveness dictated.

John Patterson was an advocate of physical fitness and every day, men and women alike were called to the gymnasium to do calisthenics in athletic garb supplied by the company. By 1905, there were five hundred women employed by the National Cash Register. Allied to fitness, John Patterson extended his jurisdiction to nutrition, and ordered certain foods to be excluded from the cafeteria menu.

At this point, his real paranoia took over. Heretofore, he held it back while he built the foundation from which to spring. Now began his compulsive firing of executives. He paid his top personnel well, in fact, he paid well all down the line, but no sooner did he hire and train a top man than he would peremptorily fire him. He became well known for this and it was claimed that one-sixth of the country's top executives had been fired by Patterson from the turn of the century to his death. Once he fired a whole department because he was displeased by their performance. His credo was "When a man becomes indispensable, fire him." Most times he didn't wait that long. This firing of top people was impulsive and his paranoia was reflected in minor ways as well. His compulsion to control became obsessive when he made rules regarding the behavior of his employees from the width of ties to the percentage of the tips they gave. He showered them with continuous memoranda which he followed up to make sure they were obeyed.

Patterson's tendencies to control and run all matters within his purvue extended to the community of Dayton. He advocated drastic changes in patronage, the management of the schools and the establishment of parks. His unsolicited advice was largely ignored but a rift with the city fathers ensued when he blamed the appalling condition of Dayton on individuals in high office and threatened to move his factory and its 38,000 workers to the east coast where they would have "decent surroundings, lower taxes and higher class visitors." Things went from bad to worse when Patterson caused a feud at NCR. He had brought from England a Charles Palmer and made him a director of the company. Palmer claimed he could read character in a person's face. This intrigued Patterson who had him scrutinize his executives and report to him. This resulted in several key men being terminated. Then Palmer issued an order to remove from the cafeteria certain foods, including bread and butter, tea and coffee, salt and pepper, etc. Hugh Chalmers, NCR's vice president tried to rescind the order so Patterson fired him along with the top sales executives.

Chalmers was furious and swore he would put Patterson behind bars. He almost succeeded were it not for a natural disaster. This confrontation stirred up articles and editorials in the newspapers criticizing Patterson, to which he responded with lawsuits. Then he shut down the factory to give him time to pursue them and thousands of workers were out of a job. This had a disastrous effect on Dayton's economy but Patterson had the upper hand, and when he was good and ready he reopened the factory and brought the workers back.

The National Cash Register Company and its product was now well established and competition sought a piece of the pie. Patterson had long decided that no one would usurp what he considered his domain—the manufacture and sales of cash registers—and handled all potential competition the same way. When an entrepreneur appeared on the horizon, he invited him to tour the Dayton plant—all expenses paid. Then he brought him into the Historical Room (called the "Gloom Room" by the employees) and showed him piles of cash registers that had been abandoned by would be competitors who had gone belly up. Then Patterson offered to buy him out. If that didn't work, he brought suit. This usually worked, for Patterson explained that litigation takes years and thousands of dollars, during which time the challenging company cannot operate.

Patterson didn't even allow a small business to deal in second hand cash registers—he had to have it all. His paranoia compelled him to set up a competing firm nearby and under sell, or he claimed violation of patent rights and brought suit. He stopped at nothing to retain supremacy in the field.

In 1912, however, Patterson and twenty-nine NCR officials were indicted for violating the Sherman Antitrust Act. All were convicted and Patterson was fined and sentenced to a year in jail. Hugh Chalmers was a key witness. Patterson was reprieved from his prison term by an Act of God. The day after Easter, the heavens opened and poured eleven inches of rain on the city, already sodden from melting snow. Patterson inspected the levees that held the three rivers that met at Dayton to form the Great Miami River and decided they would not hold. Then he took command. He ordered his carpenters to build rowboats and the bakers to bake 2,000 loaves of bread. He sent men over the country side to bring back food, beds, clothing and medical supplies. In fifteen minutes he had organized his company to cope with a disaster that had not yet occurred.

Then the levees broke and flooded the city. City government collapsed, leaving Patterson in full charge. He was in his element. He sent his two hundred and seventy-five rowboats to take stranded people off the rooftops and bring them to the factory for food and clothes and shelter and medical care. He ordered his executives in other cities to send emergency supplies and "The Cash" (as the factory was called) housed and fed them while the city recovered.

In the excitement and confusion, Patterson's conviction was forgotten. Governor James Cox, an old opponent of Patterson's, signed an order of authorization to place him at the head of the disaster efforts. Three hundred people had died and property loss was more than one hundred million dollars. Presidential representatives came to offer aid. John Patterson was a national hero.

His conviction could not be overlooked, however, and cries came for a presidential pardon. He replied in typical fashion that he did not want a pardon, he had done nothing wrong. As the city quieted down, his first act was to wire the New York Times to the effect that if the judge who tried his case set foot in Dayton Patterson would put him behind bars. One of his executives discreetly intervened and destroyed the telegram. Patterson then proceeded to mount a drive for two million dollars to pay for work on flood control, dipping deeply into his company's profits to top it off. The federal appeals court overturned the antitrust conviction and remanded another trial which never took place. Patterson went back to Dayton, welcomed by a cheering crowd. At seventy-seven, he turned the presidency over to his son Frederick, but continued to put his nose into the affairs of the company and be a general nuisance.

True to his excessive paranoid nature, however, he fired all twenty-nine of his executives who were convicted with him, blaming them "for having got me into this mess." One of these, who had been like a son to him, and his most trusted executive, the one who intercepted the telegram to the New York Times, vowed that he would build a larger business than John H. Patterson's National Cash Register, and he did. He was Thomas J. Watson, founder of IBM. John H. Patterson died at seventy-eight in 1921.

On hearing the story of John Patterson, one's first thought is, "AH! here is a benign paranoid." He was solicitous of his employees, their health and well-being. He provided nourishing meals and exercise, social outings and artistic entertainment, and gave free medical care for them and their families. All this was to benefit his company—that it remain the best and most productive. But when he came into conflict with someone who opposed him he was aggressive and unfair to the point of being almost criminal. He fired his top executives for no apparent reason and espoused unfair business practices, using any technique, no matter how unreasonable, to eliminate competitors. And he defied the anti-trust law, which was definitely illegal.

Patterson was a Dr. Jekyll and Mr. Hyde type of paranoid and true to his color, started out as a benign kind, but as success came to him in middle age he converted into a compulsive, controlling, irascible and difficult man.

PARANOIDS AS CULT LEADERS 9

 he following two stories indicate that a paranoid personality can be an inherently good person in early life, at which time the paranoid trait is submerged, showing up in middle life.

AIMEE SEMPLE McPHERSON

Aimee Elizabeth Kennedy was born in Canada in 1889 to Minnie, a Salvation Army lassie and a Methodist farmer. She was brought up by her mother to devote her life to God and was quick to learn. She seemed to have inherited this dedication and even as a young child showed signs of leadership, a strong sense of the dramatic and a headstrong, affectionate and cheerful nature.

She became involved in the Pentecostal Church and at seventeen married Robert Semple, a young preacher. They went to China as missionaries where he died, and Aimee bore a baby girl posthumously. She was broken-hearted and named her Roberta. Penniless, she returned to New York and soon married Harold McPherson, a grocery clerk. They went to Rhode Island to live with his parents and Aimee had a son, Rolf. She despaired of the life of a housewife, became depressed and fell ill. She prayed for guidance and received the answer: "Go and preach the word."

Aimee quickly regained her health, left McPherson, took the children to her mother in Canada and joined the Pentacostal group. She began lecturing, moving from town to town, slowly gathering a following. With the first donations, she bought a leaky tent which she pitched herself. The handicaps were almost unsurmountable, but nothing phased Aimee. She loved the Gypsy life and worked from dawn to dusk and thrived on it, traveling from Maine to Key West, calling on the weak, the poor, the oppressed; and they responded.

Aimee had no talent for managing money, so she called on her mother for help. Minnie joined her with the children and they shared the work and the glory. Aimee could now devote most of her time to her beloved preaching, praying and helping her flock.

Just before Christmas in 1918, Aimee, Minnie, Roberta and Rolf arrived in Los Angeles. It was wartime and there were many deprivations, but a week later, Aimee held her first revival meeting, teaching her "Foursquare Gospel": Regeneration, Divine Healing, the Second Coming of Christ and the Baptism of the Holy Ghost. She was enormously successful, contributions kept pouring in and a group of supporters built a two story house for her.

Aimee soon achieved national fame for her preaching and healing sessions as she traveled from coast to coast, stopping at the big
cities. In the meantime, Minnie took care of the children and scrimped
and saved enough money to buy a lot in Echo Park and build the
Angelus Temple. When she wasn't traveling, Aimee organized services for the needy and hungry and found jobs for the men released from
prison. Any need that went unmet, she provided for, whether it be a
Bible school, a nursery or a church paper; she even acquired her own
broadcasting station heard over thousands of miles.

She was called Sister, and wore a white flowing dress with a navy
cape, and dramatized her messages by staging performances in the
Temple with lights, costumes and flowers. They were colorful and
garish at times, but attracted attention and the congregation loved it.
While Aimee basked in the adulation of her flock, Minnie ran the
organization with an iron hand. And the money kept coming in.

By this time, both women evinced tendencies of strong paranoia.
When criticized, they laughed and terminated the membership of
those who opposed them. They had to control everything, and as the
movement grew and they prospered, signs of cruelty and disregard for
the feelings of others became evident.

Aimee Semple McPherson had two faces—Minnie always said
she had a "dual personality"—another sign of her growing paranoia.
However, she was at her peak in 1926, but this soon began to slip as her
success went to her head and her egotistical over-confidence over-
ruled. She felt all-powerful; she could do no wrong, others were
wrong, she was right—the classic course of the paranoid personality.
And her morals began to slacken, McPherson divorced her, and she
became friendly with Kenneth Orniston, who ran her radio station. He
was married and Minnie warned her that a scandal could ruin their
business, but Aimee paid no heed. She could do no wrong and felt
secure in her self-righteousness.

Aimee took a trip around the world, preaching, taking Roberta
with her and depositing her with her grandparents in Ireland. Now she
was free to have Orniston join her, which he did, and they continued
the trip. His wife sued for divorce. Aimee returned alone and soon
Orniston showed up. Back in Los Angeles, Aimee disappeared one day
while swimming. Everyone thought she had drowned, but no body
could be found. Soon, Orniston disappeared also, and the press started
rumors that they were seen together. However, after a time, he
appeared and she was found in Arizona five weeks later and said she
had been kidnapped for ransom and hidden in the desert, mistreated
and tortured. A doctor's examination revealed no signs of such an
ordeal. It was pure fabrication.

Then the story got around that Aimee and Kenneth were staying in a cottage on the beach, as he again had dropped out of sight. All this time, Minnie was furious at her daughter for creating such a scandal and for telling tall tales. Furthermore, she was demanding more and more money but never told Minnie, who was handling the finances of the Temple, how she spent it. Mother and daughter were drifting apart.

Against her mother's advice, Aimee made another tour of the United States, and this time she became friendly with the members of the press and their friends, all men and a rowdy bunch, smoking cigars and drinking whisky, which Aimee had always looked down upon. She seemed to be slipping away from Christian leanings to worldly affairs. Her paranoia was running her and she was all-powerful and right. Her success was spotty on this tour—she was not the same Aimee.

She staged a triumphant homecoming on her return to Los Angeles, floating down the aisle, smiling, her arms full of roses, a flowing robe billowing about her. A day later, she moved out of the parsonage into a rented house with the children. She wanted to get away from Minnie and her rigid principles. She played tennis and golf and listened to popular music. Everyone wondered why her mother was not with her and the press had a field day. She kept asking for more money and seemed to have changed into a worldly woman, shirking her responsibilities to God and her congregation. She bobbed her hair and drove expensive cars and wore high-priced and modish clothes. The Temple was crumbling.

Then Aimee told her mother to resign from her position as manager of the Temple, and if she refused, Aimee would resign. She had to have total control even over her mother, without whom she could never have built the Temple, or managed it so efficiently. Minnie left and Aimee took over. She was intoxicated by this new authority, and unwisely reorganized the Temple into a huge enterprise with forty branch churches. As she was running short of money, she tried to mortgage the Temple for a half million dollars for herself. Her mother talked her out of this, so she went on a tour of the British Isles. When she returned she heard that Minnie Kennedy was in trouble and was being sued by a man who claimed she reneged on an agreement to marry him. It was Minnie's turn to give the press a juicy story.

Aimee's private life was also in question, rumors abounding that she had turned to commercialism and pleasure except in the pulpit, where she was always magnificent. She was caught deceiving, telling falsehoods and squandering the Temple's money. Her paranoia was in full bloom. Minnie came back to save the sinking ship and took over the financial affairs again. The elders suspected fraud and called a grand jury to look into the matter, but when Aimee produced the books nothing could be proven and the suit was dropped. However, there was another set of books not presented in evidence made out to two fictitious names, alleged to be Aimee and Minnie.

At this time, Aimee faked a nervous breakdown, and word got around that she was gravely ill, had lost thirty pounds and was going blind. It was rumored that she had plastic surgery to remove fat, a nose job and face lift. Her followers were horrified and prayed for her soul. She went to the Caribbean to recuperate, and on her return preached on Thanksgiving over a public address system in a slow, weak voice, then fainted in a show of dramatics, drawing on everyone's sympathy. Although it was believed that she was dying, she announced that she would preach again and appeared on the arm of her son, Rolf, looking thin and wan, but beautiful in a long shimmering white gown, red roses in her arms.

Then she went on a trip around the world, mostly to escape the numerous law suits against her for large sums of money she owed. She was greeted on her return by ten thousand followers in Los Angeles, marched to the Temple in an elaborate, dramatic procession and gave the greatest performance of her career, preaching before a crowd of tens of thousands, surrounded by flowers. She was still estranged from her mother and would not see her, so Minnie moved out for good, went to the state of Washington, and married "What-a-man" Hudson, who promptly was sued for bigamy.

This was 1930, and the Wall Street crash engulfed the world. Aimee rallied and set up hot lunches, fed and housed the hungry and homeless, while ignoring the lawsuits and creditors. Then she married for the third time. David Hutton was a baritone in her choir; he was eleven years older than Aimee, and soon after the wedding was sued for breach of promise by an operator in a massage parlor. Aimee collapsed and was unconscious for an hour. The press announced that she had a fractured skull, and as she recuperated, Hutton entertained his friends around Aimee's swimming pool.

Aimee neglected the Temple for five months as she took another trip around the world, returning to announce that she would preach for eighty-three services, which she did, then took off again, leaving Hutton to run the Temple, who sued Aimee for divorce under some pretext, upon which Aimee fell ill again and was taken to the hospital. Stories about her were in the newspapers daily, and Minnie was as widely publicized. She sued "What-a-man" for divorce and after much fuss and counter-suing, Aimee's and Hutton's divorce became final. Both women vowed never to marry again.

At this point another aspect of paranoia afflicted Aimee—she became suspicious and fearful. She suspected the woman she had put in charge of the Temple of plotting to take it away from her. She feared she would lose the Temple. Dissension arose among the top command, resulting in furious allegations of fraud and deceit. Aimee shuffled the staff, firing this one and promoting that one, fighting with everyone who opposed her. There were suits and counter-suits, with Aimee always coming out on top, exerting her controlling paranoia to the full.

Aimee brought all this on herself. She had cast off her mother, alienated her daughter, been divorced by two husbands and was being bombarded by forty-five lawsuits. Her private and public life was in a shambles—through her own doing. Now she had to testify in court, which she did, playacting through it all, dressed to the nines in the latest fashion, with exotic flowers on her breast. She lied and dissembled throughout and when the judge ruled against her, fainted and was taken home by Rolf. But did she blame herself for any of her troubles? No. It was their fault, never hers.

All Aimee had left now was Rolf, her nurse and the Reverend Giles Knight, who assumed the management of the Temple, and appealed to the congregation to mortgage their homes, jewelry, all they had to save the Temple. And they did! He ran the Temple efficiently, and protected Aimee from molestations. He restricted her activities to visiting and preaching at the various branches of the church. At last Sister was cut down to size, but her appeal had deteriorated. She was frequently ill, but always gave her best; the Temple became a showplace for tourists, which helped to feed its insatiable maw. During World War II, Aimee threw herself into war work, and one day in 1944, newspaper headlines announced AIMEE IS DEAD. She had taken an overdose of a strong sedative, whether inadvertently or not will never be known. Autopsy revealed a kidney ailment, otherwise she was in good health. She was fifty-four.

This is the story of a woman who began life ostensibly a good, upright person, dedicated to helping others but who, from the beginning, showed signs of paranoia in her intense compulsion to control masses of people by her electrifying sermons. That was when she was at her best; that was what she enjoyed the most.

In the beginning, she was almost worshipped by her followers, but as time went on, her character subtly deteriorated into possessiveness and materialism, overshadowed by the compulsion to control which fathered selfishness, deceitfulness and dishonesty, and led her into excesses fostered and nurtured by her extreme paranoia.

On the face of it, you would not label Aimee Semple McPherson a paranoid personality, but that she was in an oblique sense, for her doing quality caused a deterioration of personality from that of enthusiasm and creativity into a debauchery of running off with men, lying about it, and spending a great deal of money that should have been put to better use. Aimee became engulfed in her wantonness and free living, and went along with the current making no effort to change, which demonstrated very poor self-management.

Aimee was more of a doer than a thinker. The power and control for which she strove perverted her nature, and her paranoia dominated the other facets of her personality, allowing to emerge the suspicious fearfulness, the lack of concern for others, producing a reaction of intense hostility. That hostility pervaded the rest of her life, coupled with her newfound ability to deceive, dissemble, lie and cheat, and instead of turning into cruelty, the hostility drove her to the fast living she espoused until the end and permitted her to excuse her debaucheries.

THE REVEREND JIM JONES

As we travel down the river of paranoia, the stream widens, the characters become more pronounced and take on distinctive features and different colors. Now we encounter cruelty not evident before, excessive manipulation, inordinate suspicion, total disregard and castigation of others for problems, unrestrained criticism and an overpowering urge to control all people and all situations and to eliminate whatever stands in the way to accomplish this. Now we see the wolf in sheep's clothing.

James W. Jones is described in the book GUYANA MASSACRE by Charles A. Krause, an eyewitness, as a true Jekyll-and-Hyde. Power and control were his goals under the guise of helping others. His was an extreme paranoid personality beginning in early years and extending through life, as can clearly be discerned from this brief account.

Jones was born in 1931, and facts about his childhood are conflictual. A university professor, a neighbor of the Jones family, remembers him as the "mean little six-year-old kid"—the "Dennis the Menace" of the town. When he walked by our house he shouted obscenities which shocked my mother. He often said to me: "Good morning, you son-of-a-bitch," and I would chase him."

An opposing account was printed in a local newspaper while he was studying for the ministry, obviously influenced by Jones to give a good impression. It tells of a small boy meeting a tramp who told him that he hadn't a friend in the world and had given up. Jim told him: "God is your friend and so am I," and took him home and his mother found him a job. The account goes on to state that this was a milestone in Jones' career, and led him to a life of service to humanity, especially the unfortunate. This indicates his use of manipulation early on, with the objective of building up his image as a do-gooder.

Little is recorded of his early life or of his family, except that his father was an active member of the Ku Klux Klan and his mother a factory worker. At. eighteen, he married Marceline Baldwin, a registered nurse. He enrolled in Indiana University, run by the Christian Church (Disciples of Christ), and received a B.S. in education in 1961. In the interim, he founded his church, the Christian Assembly of God, and was ordained in 1964.

Jones bought churches in Los Angeles and San Francisco and gathered a following of inner-city blacks and liberal whites, attracted by the dazzling activities of soul and gospel services, health care and good works. He made many claims, among them that he had a vision of nuclear holocaust to occur in a few years. He also claimed he could resurrect the dead and cure cancer and "psychosomatic diseases".

Jim Jones was the messiah of a terrorized but devoted congregation. They adored him and feared him. He instilled in them his paranoid fear of nuclear war, the Ku Klux Klan, racism and the CIA; and described unbelievable dark forces that would do them in. But they felt secure under his wing, that they would be saved from the holocaust and safe from the scourge of cancer and psychosomatic diseases, whatever that meant to them. The manipulation went on.

He chose to be called "Father," and said he was the spirit of Christ. At other times he was the spirit of Lenin. He was able to lecture on socialism and visions of life hereafter, inspiring his followers to pour into the Temple treasury millions of dollars worth of property, cash, social security and welfare checks.

He founded the Peoples Temple in San Francisco, and later moved it to Ukiah, California, which he considered to be the one section of the country safe from nuclear disaster, and was followed there by his brood. With one hand he extracted the life savings, meagre income and property from his followers; with the other he comforted tramps and down-and-outers and took them into the fold. Once, he used the money of the Peoples Temple to defend newsmen facing jail for refusing to reveal their sources of information, and donated a large sum to an organization to aid the elderly—Jekyll and Hyde. It is from his followers that we hear of his greed for money, cruelty, and obsession to control everything and everyone around him. He was suspicious and hostile, critical and blaming, but the side of him that thought only of others and sacrificed to help the human race was always shown to the world. Thus, he fooled those who ventured to delve into the workings of the Peoples Temple, and on the other hand maintained control over his flock through threats and reminders that the wrath of God would descend upon them if they failed to do his will.

He dabbled in politics, served on the grand jury, and to illustrate the disparity of his activities, was arrested on a lewd conduct charge of molesting an undercover policeman. The charge was dismissed on a legal technicality. He wooed celebrities, especially politicians in power, and organized missions, orphanages and soup kitchens; he adopted seven homeless children, one black, one Korean. He formed non-profit corporations and acquired various small businesses, from nursing homes to grocery stores; and the money kept pouring into the Temple's coffers. At his height, Jones had fifteen bank accounts and ten million dollars in banks in Europe, Guyana and California.

Jones exploited his good deeds and downplayed the bad, advertising his social programs: child care centers, carpentry shops, soup kitchens, and so forth. His activities encouraged articles in important newspapers and magazines, and his reputation as an evangelist and a do-gooder became widespread. He donated substantial sums of money to causes, and saw to it that this was highly publicized.

Jim Jones' paranoia was increasing, and came to a peak of suspecting persecution by certain groups in the United States. This resulted in the founding of the Peoples Temple colony in 1973 in Guyana, and the settling of "Jonestown" by his flock. In 1976, Jones was named "Humanitarian of the Year" by the Los Angeles Herald, and one of the hundred most outstanding clergymen in the nation by an inter-faith organization. Mayor Moscone appointed him to the San Francisco Housing Authority, and a year later he became its chairman. That same year, he received the Martin Luther King, Jr. Humanitarian Award.

Jones traveled back and forth from California to Jonestown, but spent most of his time in Guyana, managing his followers and haranguing them with his distorted beliefs, such as cancer cures and other deceptive claims. He staged bizarre displays of extracting cancers from a victim, using the organs of animals as props, and other strange and grisly shows, pronouncing the tricks as miracles he performed.

There were dissenters who attempted to tell their stories to the authorities, and if these warnings had been taken seriously, the frightful mass murders might have been prevented. But Jones had built up a reputation of sanctity under the guise of religious convictions, and wooed and won the support of key political figures who believed him and considered the allegations to be false.

At this point, rumors of dissatisfaction arose among some of the members, and one cultist who announced he was leaving the Temple was found murdered the next day. Derogatory accounts about the cult were published and an official investigation was requested, but refused by Mayor Moscone. The Temple was sued in 1977 for a million dollars by Al and Jeanne Mills, who said they were beaten and cheated out of their property by Jones, and several relatives of other cult members issued a statement which was published in the press accusing Jones of human rights violations. Another former member filed an affidavit testifying to conditions at Jonestown, and warned of suicide rehearsals and pacts. Another suit was filed by James Cobb charging that Jones was plotting "mass murder" which included young children, and planning collective suicide. United States consular officials in Guyana visited Jonestown four times, but could find no complaints or evidence of mistreatment.

Jones' episodes of bizarre behavior became increasingly numerous and caused one after another of his flock to see through the chicanery and withdraw from his influence. Those who followed him to Jonestown, however, had no choice but to stay.

By 1977, Jones had settled firmly in Guyana, never to return, and members who had left the Temple ran an article in the magazine New West and the San Francisco Chronicle. It told of the beatings, the extortions and the humiliating rites of the Temple. This released a flood of revelations by others who had been afraid to speak out. It also generated many civil suits against Jones, claiming fraud, divestiture of large sums of money and even the entrapment of their children and loved ones.

It revealed a private world of nightmares which Jones ruled as "Father." He imposed a regimen of terror, physical punishment, beatings, exhaustion, emotional dependency and tyranny. He enticed his people with his charismatic hold, then reduced them to abject poverty, fear, grinding labor and punishment. He held meetings at which he exerted his hypnotic influence, whipped them into a religious frenzy, then stripped away their egos one by one through humiliation, beating and denunciation. If anyone even slightly protested, that person was brought up before the audience and savagely beaten. This cruelty extended to women and even children—no one escaped.

Sex played a major role in Jones' command. He used it as a reward or a punishment, as he saw fit, in order to obtain total control of the lives under him—also to gratify his sexual appetite. Sex was Jones' tool for domination and blackmail. His secretary set up sexual liaisons with men as well as women for him, while at the same time he ordered horrible public punishment of men accused or suspected of homosexual tendencies. In fact, Jones proclaimed himself "the only legitimate object of sexual desire" and engaged in six-hour sessions of sexual activity and boasted about it.

One keen observer relates the sinister, subtle changes in Jones' personality and style as the years progressed. This mirrors the classic progress of paranoia as the individual ages: Jones' "do-gooding" days in the beginning, his slow downgrading of values showing up in subtle ways, then the utter degradation of his morals, and increasing tendencies to control and dominate those who remained with him. The slightest disagreement with his orders was regarded as "treason" and the perpetrator dealt with accordingly.

Suspiciousness greatly increased also. Jones was convinced he and his followers were in the center of a conspiracy, and blamed the CIA, the United States Government and other malignant forces he could not identify. He claimed that they would prosecute, torture, imprison and kill anyone who did not obey him.

He was irrational in his thinking, often held meetings of his followers and raved for hours. It was never quite clear whether he used these harangues to manipulate his flock or that he was unable to distinguish fantasy from reality.

Jim Jones had a strange hold over his followers, a diabolical force that transcended all human interactions. His total disregard for human life and feelings was exchanged for indescribable, vicious cruelty. His power came from fear, guilt and fatigue, as he forced them to go without sleep all night; and work hard the next day—night after night, day after day. He coerced his minions to perform unbelievable acts of brutality while he watched, and ordered his guards to hold him back from inflicting greater harm, while he witnessed savage beatings with obvious relish. Some of his victims were children, four and five years old, and he yelled at those who beat them to beat them harder.

In November of 1978, United States Congressman Leo Ryan of California left with an entourage of officials, newsmen and relatives of cultists to investigate the Peoples Temple at Jonestown. He and four others were shot dead at the airport, and eleven others were wounded.

At five o'clock on that Saturday, November 18th, Jones gave the order, and he and his followers took cyanide. He had rehearsed them many times. Nine hundred died; the massacre was total.

Could it be that Jim Jones took his cue from Aimee Semple McPherson as he plotted his paranoid future? Could he have observed from her experience that the way to achieve power, money and control is to be an evangelist? Aimee formed a "Temple" in Los Angeles; a few years later he did also.

THE CARGO CULTS

These cults illustrate that paranoid leaders emerge not only in civilized but also in developing countries where they seize on the benevolence of the industrialized nations to attract and control their followers. A paranoid personality is exhibited by someone who is driven by a need for power and control and evolves into a politico-religious leader. These cults suggest that this kind of person, although uncommon, is prevalent in every culture. When one appears, he pushes himself into areas such as religion and politics where he can control masses of people. Thus, he gains power where no one can challenge him and he can satisfy his personal needs by instilling fear, manipulating to get his way, and displaying all the identifiable traits of paranoia.

It is amazing how many people go along with the demands of a cult leader as he distorts religious beliefs to get what he wants, and develops a technique to get rid of people who challenge him or pose a threat.

The "cargo" cults first emerged in Melanesia in the South Pacific on the Island of Fiji, with the arrival of explorers: Tasman in 1643, Cook in 1774 and Bligh in 1792. They were started by a "leader" with that indefinable quality of charisma, and spread as the white man explored one island after another bringing civilization and various religions, deadly implements of war and diseases previously unknown. They burgeoned with the world wars, and many islands still abound in them.

Cult leaders are strongly paranoid with intense desire to control. They begin by attracting a small audience, which grows into a following, then a movement and finally an organization. They gain authority by the ability to deliver a message that is powerful and believable, and is contrived to coincide with their own objectives. Here is an example.

In 1932 on Buka, a quasi-religious movement sprang up under the leadership of Pako, who told the villagers that a cargo (thus the name for this cult) ship would be arriving soon, but first, there would be a tidal wave. The natives believed him, stopped working, and fled to the hills. Pako claimed that one of the prophets had gone to heaven and St. Peter told him to persuade the people to go to church regularly, give up their dances and rituals, ask for higher wages and levy tolls from the Whites. Then they should renounce Christianity, sacrifice pigs to the ancestors and worship them. He preached that the natives would be equal to the Whites and they should build warehouses to hold the stores that the cargo ships will bring. They did this and Buka was united for the first time. Here Pako's paranoia paid off as he controlled the natives and exerted his power to persuade them to follow his orders. But his power of persuasion was overbearing—he went too far. In order to gain time, Pako went abroad where he adopted European ways and brought them back to Buka. Then he built a modern house for himself and his family.

Soon a trading vessel arrived, and the natives had to be prevented forcibly from carrying off the cargo. They insisted it was theirs, and the White crew their ancestors. Pako was arrested and exiled to Nadang where he died. However this did not end the movement. Sanop, a leader from another village, witnessed what Pako was able to do and planned his strategy to take over the movement. He fell into a trance and prophesied that the cargo ship would come, and the natives would rule Buka. When it didn't arrive, he said it was because there was plenty of pig and taro to eat, and it would come when that had gone. He predicted a "darkness" followed by an earthquake, so the people rushed to build low houses. By Good Friday, there still was no cargo and the island settled down.

But Sanop did not rest. He was possessed by his paranoia and had to hold on to his power over the people, so he concocted this story. He told them—and they believed him—that Pako had risen from the dead and was working on the arrival of the cargo ship. He said he heard a man's voice coming from Pako's house announcing that he could perform miracles. Crowds rushed to be baptized, and to ensure the arrival of the ship, cleaned the cemeteries and bedecked them with flowers, and tidied the shacks.

The movement became strongly anti-European and plans to kill the "invaders" were discussed. Sanop promised rifles and planes and men began drilling for battle. "Into the sea with the Whites!" was the cry. The Europeans were accused of the non-arrival of the cargo, and the unrest reached a climax as the people anticipated its coming, the takeover of government and rule by the natives. There was an earth tremor on Buka, and the laborers deserted. Then the government acted, they burned Pako's house, but Sanop escaped. However, his rule as leader was over.

The natives were still waiting for the "coming", and believed that the Germans would send the cargo, but that hope was dashed with the arrival of the Japanese, who by December 1942 had organized Buka into a military base. Soldiers, messengers and police were trained the Japanese way. Work teams were set up and the natives had to cultivate gardens for all to share. This was forced labor to them, and they resented it. They found out that the Japanese were stealing their food, and they were soon reduced to starvation, aided by the allied bombing. The arrival of the Americans several years later brought order out of chaos.

All these movements adhered to similar principles; to renounce social distinctions and worldly wealth, to share property, to practice asceticism and austere behavior. This emphasized democratic solidarity but meant giving up enjoyment in life. The persistence of these movements indicates that the failure of a prophecy doesn't destroy the people's belief, but seems to strengthen it. Failures are interpreted in many ways, as blaming the Europeans or the Japanese—indicating an element of paranoia. The fact that the spirits did not appear did not prove they don't exist, but confirms that they do. So the cults and movements thrived.

PARANOIDS IN GOVERNMENT

10

JOHN EDGAR HOOVER

A paranoid personality doesn't always mean an unpleasant person and he or she can be a dedicated, constructive and creative individual. Paranoids are usually perfectionistic and driven. John Edgar Hoover was such—exacting and self-disciplined, and he expected those who worked for him to be likewise.

Hoover was born on New Year's Day 1895 in Washington, D. C. He had one brother, Dickerson, fifteen years his senior. His family of Swiss stock settled in the early 1800s in Washington's southeast; the solid, stone house was a sign of the family's station—middle echelon government and middle income. Their father was an official in the United States Geodetic Survey; their mother, Annie, was the dominating influence in the family, a strong, pious woman of uncompromising morality, who brought up her children with strict, disciplinary precepts.

Edgar was a good student, bright, diligent and a perfectionist. He was ambitious and started earning money at the age of twelve. He chose the best high school, walking there six miles, and a curriculum that far exceeded the requirements, graduating at the top of his class. His light weight excluded him from most sports, but he distinguished himself on the debating team and as captain of the cadet corps. He received a scholarship to the University of Virginia, but could not afford it, so took a job at the Library of Congress and went to George Washington University night law school, graduating in 1917 with a B.A. and an M.A. in law.

Hoover took a position as a law clerk at the Justice Department and worked tirelessly long hours. The First World War had broken out and he became aware of the subversive acts being carried out by German secret agents in the United States against the export of munitions to the Allies. At that time, there were no laws against this. Soon the United States entered the war and the country was in a turmoil. The meagre number of agents of the Federal Bureau of Investigation had to cope with millions of enemy aliens, draft dodgers, spies and saboteurs, as well as militant pacifists. The armistice of 1918 did not bring an end to the crises, for the price of food had doubled and strikes were rampant in just about every service and industry.

To add to the chaos, the Russian revolution touched deeply into the fabric of the country, with terrorist acts of bombings and threats to many of the top officials of the Federal government. The Bolsheviks and the I.W.W. were shaking the country to the core. Attorney General Mitchell Palmer created a General Intelligence Division of Investigation under Hoover, his special assistant, to study subversion and to make recommendations. Hoover went after Communists and radicals who fomented revolution, such as the I.W.W. and other groups who were trying to form a revolutionary labor movement.

At one time, Hoover was labeled a racist because the Communists were trying to whip the Negroes into revolutionary activity, and set aside part of the South for a Negro "republic". These accusations, however, proved to be nothing but political backbiting which the Attorney General also shared. Hoover continued to round up and deport Communists and other trouble makers including those responsible for the assassination of President McKinley and Henry Clay Frick. Matters were well in hand until the bombing in Wall Street in which thirty-eight people were killed and fifty-seven injured. The year was 1920.

Hoover went into action under orders from the Attorney General and drew up plans for dragnet raids to gather all aliens with membership in the Communist Parties and deport them. This was going well until president Harding came into office and changed the top leadership, appointing cronies of his who were ineffectual and demoted Hoover. The Ku Klux Klan became active in the South and lynchings, torture and brutality increased dramatically. Hoover bypassed his superiors and took control into his own hands and, his paranoia working for the good, cleaned up the terrorism. Harding died and Calvin Coolidge became President. The country was finally on its way to law and order when Coolidge appointed Harlan Fiske Stone as Attorney General.

Stone appointed Hoover head of the F.B.I. in 1924. Hoover accepted but only under certain conditions: that he be permitted to draw up strict rules and regulations. Stone agreed. Hoover decreed that the Bureau must be divorced from politics and responsible only to the Attorney General. He stipulated that appointments to the Bureau be based on merit, promotions on proven ability only, and his men be trained in law and accounting. And he wanted a free hand to build the Bureau to meet his standards of the highest moral principles. Now Hoover could run his Bureau as he saw fit. He had total control and he was content.

The activities of the Bureau were to be limited to functions confined to Federal law violations and answerable to the Attorney General, and Hoover was to be free to fire those he considered incompetent, political appointees. He quickly got rid of the corrupt and undesirable, and advised his agents that the Bureau was to operate solely on the basis of efficiency. He set up field offices with Special Agents in charge. He established a system of performance and a routine he expected his agents to adhere to. He was tough and demanding of others, and insisted on absolute secrecy in regard to all activities of the Bureau. The FBI was soon looked up to as the best law enforcement agency in the world.

It was 1928, and Prohibition was the law of the land. Bootlegging became a major enterprise and a main source of funds for the underworld of organized crime. Criminals also profited from gambling, robbery, prostitution and dope peddling. Hoover was distressed that this lawlessness was not under Federal jurisdiction. He asked Attorney General Stone if he could move in and Stone said: "Go ahead." Hoover did and heads began to roll. The case that put the FBI on the map was the kidnapping of the Lindbergh baby, and the subsequent arrest and conviction of Bruno Hauptman.

In 1935, the Federal Bureau of Investigation became official and agents were permitted to carry guns, so Hoover started a school of combat training for his agents. He involved himself in the details of every case and directed many investigations leading to conviction. He had to know that each one was handled to perfection. His paranoia was driving him far beyond the necessary supervision. The Bureau was his life—an extension of himself. Successful as Hoover was, he was not without enemies from various segments of the Government and society. He was not an easy man to work with and the principles to which he expected all to conform were rigid. He was under fire by the Ku Klux Klan and radical newspaper columnists, as well as some members of Congress who disliked him and his Bureau and took every opportunity to shoot him down at congressional hearings. He was not well liked and was criticized personally, especially as he considered his battle against crime a moral crusade and would not condone the slightest leaning toward toleration of criminality.

Franklin D. Roosevelt was in the White House, but Hoover was not slated to operate smoothly within the Washington bureaucracy. Some members of the New Deal wanted him out, Postmaster General James Farley in particular, but Hoover stood his ground, feeling secure that what he was doing was right, and President Roosevelt backed him up.

As this story unfolds, you may be wondering what is paranoid about this dedicated, upright young man who is doing such a magnificent job for his country. John Edgar Hoover's paranoia is manifested in his determination to control the Bureau, his refusal to accept the criticism leveled at him by the Congress, and his suspicion of everyone who did not support him. His paranoia worked for good, not evil. As a young man, his idealism was stronger than his hostility. Only as he aged, did it develop into over-suspicion and hostility of a vindictive nature.

In 1940, World War II raged in Europe and the President asked Hoover to take over the highly confidential job of the surveillance of Communists, Fascists and subversive activists. This meant training his agents for espionage, which was not easy. Again, he insisted that he be free from political control. He was correct in this decision when the United States entered the war, but the privilege left him open to attack by other agencies which were jealous and fought him tooth and nail. He was most successful, however, and used the infiltration method of investigation to identify agents within the government who were engaged in Soviet and Japanese espionage. Then came the bombing of Pearl Harbor. Hoover was given the handling of press censorship and counterespionage in which the FBI was deeply engaged throughout the war. He took a chance and set up two German refugees as double agents. Both proved to be enormously successful in rounding up spies and cracking spy rings, working both ends against the middle. The Germans were totally confused. By the 1944 invasion of Normandy, the FBI, with British intelligence, had brought Nazi espionage to a standstill.

Regardless of his success, however, Hoover's frustration was mounting. The function of the FBI was to gather information and not to act upon it. He had been keeping an eye on Communists since 1936, but was ignored when he reported espionage within the OSS (Office of Strategic Services), and discovered that secrets of the Manhattan project—the atomic bomb—were being passed along to the Russians. Although they were considered allies, Hoover didn't trust them. But his warnings fell on deaf ears and top government officials repeatedly failed to expose and expel from government service those whom he had designated as Communists.

This story is now history, and those involved in betraying the United States finally brought to justice, but too late. The most familiar names are Ethel and Julius Rosenberg, Alger Hiss, Harry Dexter White and Elizabeth Bentley. Whittaker Chambers was the "good guy" who finally was able to implicate the "bad guys" by his now famous "pumpkin papers." The controversy raged on, and none of the government officials, not even President Truman, would listen to or believe John Edgar Hoover, who knew the truth and was helpless to act, his healthy suspicions engulfed in the deluge of bureaucratic dominance from higher up.

Hoover spoke out on the system of probation and parole as too permissive, and deplored the maladministration of those in charge. Of the first three hundred of the most wanted list of criminals, two hundred and thirty-four had received judicial leniency or special favors. They were all repeat offenders. Groups began to attack him from all sides—it seemed as though they had nothing else to do. They claimed he was anti-Negro and anti-Semitic, yet an investigation could prove neither. Then President Truman issued an order to investigate everyone in the Federal employ for connection with Communists or subversives. Hoover was accused of conducting a witch hunt, but was solidly backed by the President and Attorney General. It was a trying time, however.

During the 1940s, Hoover often appeared before the House Committee on Un-American Activities to report on communism and subversive acts. He often supplied members of Congress information on individuals holding important posts within government who were obviously communistic or subversive and suspected of endangering the national security, but this was never acted upon. So when Senator Joseph R. McCarthy began his campaign against communists in government, Hoover applauded his efforts, and they became fast friends. McCarthy did all he could to follow up on Hoover's investigations, which had been neglected for so many years, but the story of Joe McCarthy is history and does not belong here.

After the war, different problems plagued Hoover. A new type of crime became pandemic, emanating from all classes, especially among young people, caused in part, according to Hoover, by the disintegration of the family. He concentrated on juvenile crime and delinquency, and urged the formation of boys' clubs. He gave lectures to ParentTeachers Associations, the Boy Scouts and church groups, and especially he stressed the importance of parental influence. In the fifties and sixties he observed the increase in affluence and its permissiveness, the relaxation of the codes of ethics and morality. He deplored the use of marijuana and the widespread sexual promiscuity— the sexual revolution. He watched the crime figures rise and justified the trend by the moral decay that had set in, and that many law-abiding citizens were willing to compromise their ideals if an easy dollar could be made.

John Edgar Hoover served under ten presidents and got along with most of them, although he couldn't understand why Truman tolerated subversives in his administration and never knew where he stood with Eisenhower. He was aware that John Kennedy and Bobby Kennedy wanted to get him out of office, however his friends in the Congress prevented that, but his troubles really began when Jack Kennedy made Bobby Attorney General. When Kennedy was assassinated, the FBI was blamed for not preventing it!

President Johnson and Hoover had been friends and neighbors for a long time and Johnson staunchly supported him, but could not stop the attacks by Bobby Kennedy, who harassed Hoover endlessly in an effort to force his resignation. Kennedy ordered him about like a lackey and talked him down to his men in the department. He set up a group of agents to do investigative work under him, and went over Hoover's head ordering agents to do this and that without alerting Hoover. And he circulated false stories about the Bureau and leaked them to the press.

Rumors that Hoover was homosexual were picked up by the press during the time of the onslaughts by Bobby Kennedy and those who did not like him and wanted him out of office. Although he never married, this is not true. Undoubtedly, his dedication to the Bureau negated all thought of marriage and devoting time to a wife and family. In fact, he had little personal life, although he had many friends, both men and women.

During this time, Bobby Kennedy broke many Federal statutes as though he were above the law, and acted in a brash, bad-mannered and undisciplined way. Hoover was shocked at the drunken parties and sexual escapades of the Kennedy brothers, and the harassment went on. He was openly criticized as the civil rights movement spread throughout the southern states. He was accused of wiretapping Martin Luther King's telephone which he had not done, but he kept an eye on King because of his association with underground Communist officials. A few years later they came to terms with one another and a clearer understanding. Then King was assassinated and Hoover tracked down his killer—that same day came word of the assassination of Robert Kennedy. The battle between two paranoid personalities came to an end.

It was 1970, Hoover was seventy-five years old and it appeared that most of the administration and Congress wanted him out of office. There were attacks on his age, his health, and the way he ran the Bureau. He was attacked in the press and in political periodicals, and he countered each attack with a vitriolic protest, every derogatory remark with forceful explanatory denials. His paranoia was trying to protect him with full force, but its rebuttals only seemed to exacerbate his enemies to more vicious onslaughts.

Then two of Hoover's agents turned against him and gave spurious information about the Bureau and Hoover's personal life to the press. All was false, but Senator George McGovern and Senator Edward Kennedy got into the act, followed by Vice-President Spiro Agnew. Although an investigation of the Bureau was launched, nothing could be proved against it or Hoover's management, but the furor roared on, encouraged by the press.

The "dump Hoover" movement was kept alive by the New York Times and the Washington Post, assisted by Representative Hale Boggs, who demanded Hoover's resignation on the floor of the House. What he blamed Hoover for blew up in his face, for he couldn't prove anything, but the press kept plugging, even though the accusations had no substance. Then Johnson appointed Ramsay Clark as Attorney General—the worse thing he could have done to his friend, but Johnson was having his own troubles. Clark's policies diametrically opposed Hoover's. He believed that the victim is more responsible than the aggressor in a criminal case!

The election of Richard Nixon as President did not change things and Clark kept trying to destroy Hoover. When he found that he could not get him out of office, he went at it tooth and nail. The following year, President Nixon jumped in and stopped the harassment of Hoover, backing him solidly with his office. Hoover was seventy-seven on New Year's Day 1972 and on May Day night, he died in his sleep of hypertensive cardiovascular disease. He lay in state in the Capitol Rotunda—an honor accorded only to twenty-one other American heroes and statesmen. President Nixon extolled him as "one of the giants of our times."

INDIRA NEHRU GANDHI

This famous lady was very young when she showed paranoid tendencies as she made speeches to her friends in her grandfather's garden and, at the age of seven, organized the youth movement for the cause of independence. The thread of developing paranoia can be traced as her life unfolds; the thirst for power, then the reach, the need to control, the breakdown of ethical values, the suspicion, the hostility and finally the cruelty.

Indira Nehru was born in 1917 to Jawaharlal and Kamala in Allahabad. The Nehrus were Brahmins from Kashmir and had achieved social prominence and equality with the British. Indira's grandfather was Motilal Nehru, a lawyer, and he built Anand Bhavan, a big house on a huge estate where he entertained lavishly. Indira grew up in this luxurious milieu.

The Nehrus became friendly with Mahatma Mohandas Gandhi and adopted his ideology of gaining independence from the British through peaceful means. This involved eschewing the European way of life which they had enjoyed for many years and reverting to the simple Indian dress and social structure.

Indira was indoctrinated at an early age into the world of politics and joined her family in the total commitment to the cause of independence. She didn't play as other children did but organized war games with her friends, and harangued them standing on a wooden table in the garden—preaching the quest for independence.

When Indira was twelve, she organized the Monkey Brigade of boys and girls who worked as volunteers for the cause, addressing envelopes, running errands, making flags, delivering messages and so forth. She was very lonely during this period as her parents were extremely busy and were in and out of jail, pursued by the British for their subversive activities. Her education was interrupted several times as she was switched from a European school in Geneva to an Indian school, and then tutored at home. In due course, she went to the university where a broad curriculum included the arts and nature studies. Her mother died of tuberculosis and she was transferred to Oxford in England where she met Feroze Gandhi, her future husband.

It was 1939, the Nazis were advancing and Indira returned to India with Feroze. This ended her formal education, but she was where she wanted to be—to work for the beloved cause to which she was dedicated.

She announced that she would marry Feroze but there was dissension because of the diversity of their backgrounds and the difference in their religions; Feroze came from modest means, Indira was brought up in luxury, but her mind was made up and they were married in 1942. She was twenty-four. Their first son, Rajiv, was born in 1944, their second in 1946. She had an English governess for the children and was busy helping her father, the Prime Minister. She ran his household, acted as secretary, nurse and his official hostess. This was her apprenticeship for her future career and, as Jawarlalal's companion, she visited the United States, China, the Soviet Union and France. The experience proved invaluable.

Indira Gandhi was elected to the Congress Working Committee in 1955, then to its presidency. Feroze suffered a heart attack and died in 1960, and her father at seventy was showing signs of age. Indira was shouldering more and more of the responsibility of his office.

Nehru died in 1964 after having suffered several strokes. Although it was expected, Indira was stunned at his death, and went into retirement. She lost interest in politics. Shastri was chosen prime minister and persuaded Indira to join his government, which she finally did. She became more and more involved and proved to be a forceful and successful ambassador in times of upheaval and dissension.

In 1966, Shastri died suddenly of a heart attack, and a general election was called. Several men ran for the office of prime minister and Indira's friends put her name in nomination. She won with 355 votes—more than any other candidate, becoming the nation's first female prime minister.

Indira Gandhi had few administrative skills, but she was a forceful and inspiring speaker. However, during the first few months of her administration she demonstrated weakness and vacillation. As she formed her Cabinet, she met opposition from those who questioned her sagacity and experience, and when matters of great concern were put before her, she often made hasty decisions, acting on her intuition rather than thorough research. She was often criticized, but claimed she was right—the others were wrong. Her paranoia was emerging. She felt an urge to control the members of the Cabinet and to impose her views on them without listening to theirs.

Eventually, every move Indira made was opposed by members of the Cabinet, who were trying to curb her freedom as prime minister. She drew further and further into herself. There was no one on whom she could depend for counsel; her father and Feroze were gone, and Gandhi had long since been assassinated. The Parliament met daily, and she experienced heckling and disruption from members of the opposition parties, sometimes from her own. Allegations of misdeeds, taunts, abuse and personal ridicule were hurled at her.

The prime minister built up her defenses by gathering close friends and family members upon whom she could depend for support. The group was called the "kitchen cabinet", and Indira kept tight control over its members, dismissing any who showed the slightest sign of exploiting his position. She visited the United States and was warmly received by President Lyndon B. Johnson, but several actions she took later displeased him, and she lost favor and received threats and criticism. Both were strong-willed, paranoid leaders and neither would bend.

The 1967 general elections found Indira on the campaign trail, forceful and confident. She was finally coming into her own, emerging from shyness and low self-esteem. Despite bitter opposition, she won the election. The London Sunday Times named Indira the "Most Powerful Woman in the World," yet she continued to have trouble with members of her Cabinet until she appointed Desai deputy prime minister. They worked fairly well together, with Desai providing the talents Indira lacked; they were a good team, yet her paranoid personality precluded complete accord and they continued to have differences, which added to the existing opposition of the Syndicate.

In essence, Indira Gandhi was a liberal opposed to the conservative Old Guard, of which Desai was a member. She had only minority support in parliament, so she advanced the elections by a year to ensure that her Congress Party could win enough seats to form a stable government. The strategy worked, and she chose her cabinet without interference. The Old Guard was defeated, her self-confidence surged; she felt a formidable sense of power. However, the infighting continued, Indira never knowing which member of her Cabinet was trying to get her out of office, and who was hobnobbing with whom, working behind her back to unseat her.

So she tightened the reins of her authority and placed directly under her the Central Bureau of Investigation and the prestigious Home portfolio. Her control was building. Indira exercised her paranoia in this fashion, and any member of her political family who tried to encroach on her territory got his knuckles rapped. She was in complete command, and inevitably the press and her enemies spread rumors that she was overstepping her authority. The polls showed her popularity waning, but Indira was learning that politics is the art of acquiring, holding and wielding power. She had become expert in its use, and learned that success is due to planning, conspiracy, surprise and ruthlessness. Her paranoia burgeoned.

Then came a real blow. Indira Gandhi was indicted on charges of corruption in connection with the 1971 elections. The news was sensational and her followers gathered around her. She was asked to resign by the High Court, but she held fast and her supporters rose up in arms against the judiciary. Indira stood her ground pending appeal, which proved unnecessary as she declared India under a second Emergency—the first was in existence since the Bangladesh war. A state of emergency is virtual dictatorship by the ruling party. It was declared overnight, without the knowledge of the Cabinet members, some of whom were agitating to remove her. But it worked and she assumed absolute power.

Indira explained her action in a standard speech she had sent about the country that there was a "plot" to overthrow the government and remove her from office. Her emergency powers wiped out the judgment against her and conferred immunity on her, the president and others in high office in regard to past and future criminal offenses. These pronouncements were tantamount to amendments to the constitution and an Act of parliament. Thus Indira Gandhi had control over the press and the opposition. Censorship was instituted and a code of ethics for journalists and editors. She had the right to pass laws overriding fundamental rights and forbidding "anti-national associations and activity." This amounted to overall rule by the national government.

In essence, Indira Gandhi created a police state. How was this justified? How was this enacted? There was shocking brutality and torture toward political dissenters. Mrs. Gandhi denied all knowledge of cruelty or force. Arrests were arbitrary, atrocities were brought to her attention, but were ignored. Thousands were arrested and jailed without trial. People were afraid, therefore obedient; censorship kept them ignorant of events. Surprise visits were made to check on government employees and snoop on what they were doing. It was a totalitarian government. The cruelty of her paranoia was clearly apparent.

In her speeches, Indira Gandhi depicted herself as a gentle, humble and kind person who could never think of hurting anyone. She didn't look for success or power, only to serve the people. She launched publicity on her "dynamic decade" of accomplishments, and had books published and exhibitions displayed of her achievements for the people. A series of civil disasters took place, a flood devastated a village, a mine disaster killed four hundred workers—the government did nothing, acting as though it had not happened. Indira's behavior was one of deceptions and manipulations. She had total disregard for the feelings of others, and appeared to have no compassion.

And what had Mrs. Gandhi achieved during this decade? The large industries increased their assets by 150%, big business flourished; production, savings, capital spending and investment in the public sector declined. The government received large sums of money as foreign aid, but none went toward land reform which was badly needed. The "emergency" did nothing for the masses; only the prosperous benefitted.

Indira Gandhi believed in dynastic rule as in the British Empire, and was determined that one of her sons follow her as prime minister. Rajiv, the eldest, was not interested in politics so she began to groom Sanjay, even though she was well aware of his irresponsibility, lack of training and reprehensible behavior. She kept repeating "I am a democrat," which she never was; she was merely reiterating the long held desire of Mahatma Gandhi and her father to bring democracy to India.

India's sixth national election was a referendum on one issue, i.e., would the Congress Party receive a mandate to continue the dictatorship of Mrs. Gandhi? For the first time she and her party were soundly defeated. This was 1977. She and Sanjay tried to recoup her power and build up the strength of the Congress Party, but he was extremely unpopular, especially as he was investigating the Janata Government in power and found illegal and criminal conduct which brought about its collapse in 1979. Mrs. Gandhi reorganized her party as Congress I and won the election! She was back in power, having been assisted by large corporations with which she had maintained associations. It was 1980.

Sanjay did more to injure his mother's reputation through his shady business dealings than any of her opponents. He was unscrupulous and lacked intellectual capacity and business acumen. In 1980, he died in a plane crash at the age of thirty-three. The country heaved a sigh of relief.

Mrs. Gandhi turned to her older son, Rajiv, and organized a campaign to draft him as the heir-apparent. He was not interested, and preferred to pursue his career as a pilot for Indian Airlines, but in deference to his mother and the country, he had to make a decision. He entered the political scene amidst rampant inflation, high unemployment, corruption, crime and brutality—inexperienced, a babe in the woods.

The brief reign of the Janata government had effected much

needed change; during those two years the country experienced the greatest growth it had ever known. Democracy and human rights were being adopted. With Indira's reinstatement, things went back to square one—a centralized rule with an authoritarian superstructure of government. She had to control all.

There are several religious sects in India, one of which is the Sikh ideology of fifteen million people, who prayed at the shrine of the Golden Temple in the holy city of Amritsar. The shrine was a base for terrorists in their struggle against the Indian government, and many terrorist attacks came from there. Prime Minister Gandhi ordered the base destroyed, the Golden Temple was decimated and five hundred Sikhs were killed. On October 31st, 1984, five months later, Indira Gandhi was assassinated by two of her Sikh bodyguards. Rajiv succeeded her as prime minister.

HUEY PIERCE LONG, JR.

People with strong paranoid trends often choose politics as a career. Although Indira Gandhi was born into politics, Huey Long did not hesitate to choose the field upon his first exposure. But unlike Indira, whose paranoia was barely visible when she was young, Huey knew as a teenager what he wanted—control and power. As you follow the trend in tandem you will see that in middle life it reaches its peak.

Huey Pierce Long, Jr. was born in 1893 in Winnfield, Louisiana, one of eight brothers and sisters. He had a comfortable childhood. His father was a successful farmer and landowner, but Huey did not take to farmwork and spent his time in pursuits that pleased him. He was bright, opinionated, outspoken, restless, and extremely self-centered. He read a lot and won a prize debating on the high school team. When he was fourteen, he worked on the campaign of a candidate for governor and his life's goal was established—politics.

His formal education ended in 1910 when he left school to travel as a salesman, but gave it up as it earned him little. He became engaged to Rose McConnell, and told her that he would run for state office, then for governor of Louisiana, then United States senator, then for the presidency—and would win them all. His egoism showed up early in life—a mark of excessive paranoia.

He wanted to study law to further his political ambitions, so he borrowed money from his brother Julius, and enrolled in Tulane law school, passed a special examination and moved back to Winnfield to practice. Huey and Julius didn't get along, so Huey moved to a one-room office where business gradually picked up and he could earn enough to support his family with part-time work as a traveling salesman. He had an affinity for the underdog—the small man—and this was evident in his practice. Once in a while he took a corporate case, but he told the truth when he said later that he had never taken a case against a poor man.

True to his prophecy, he assumed his first political office at the age of twenty-five as Public Service Commissioner. He worked hard, challenging the antiquated laws and practices long discarded by other states. By 1923, he was ready to run for governor. His motto was "first you come into power, then you do things." He campaigned long and hard, frantically attacking the incumbents and the corporations, upholding the little man. He lost, but he showed surprising strength at the polls. It was a beginning.

He ran again in 1928, having built up his public image to the point that he was known and recognized in every hamlet and town in Louisiana. He campaigned tirelessly, never pausing to rest—and won. At thirty-five, Huey Long was Governor of Louisiana. His rural vote was conclusive; small farmers voted for him, wealthy farmers did not.

Now the flies began to flock to the honey, as Long was relatively unknown. What would he do as governor? The old guard muscled in and tried to win him over; they entertained him, flattered him and gave him expensive gifts. They were appalled, however, at his inaugural scene as his followers arrived in buggies, carts, on mules and on foot—tobacco-chewing farmers with their sunbonneted wives, dancing to country music and jazz on a platform Long had set up. The conservatives were aghast. Right away Huey used his paranoia to place total power at his fingertips at all levels of government. He forced legislation that gave him control of all departments, and intimidated the legislature into supporting his programs.

Unquestionably, he did good for the state. He provided free textbooks for the schools; paved the highways; brought cheap natural gas to New Orleans despite opposition. He revised the state tax codes to help the poor and increased the burden on the oil and gas interests, but when he proposed a levy of five cents on every barrel of petroleum refined in the state to offset a budget deficit, it boomeranged. His opponents and the oil group voted to impeach him on a number of charges.

He fought back by calling a mass meeting of his supporters and told them that Standard Oil and its wealthy friends were trying to scuttle his programs for the people. Then he induced enough senators through intimidation to vote against impeachment and it was thrown out.

Next he proceeded to take measures to gain more power. Huey Long built his machine on patronage—the giving and taking away of state jobs. Thus he could control every office, and at the slightest sign of disloyalty, he withdrew patronage. The entire bureaucracy was so threatened it became subservient to him. Even the courts were dragged in through threats, pressure and gerrymandering. His methods were devious and often cruel—flaunting his paranoia.

He used the radio lavishly, announcing his programs to help the people and denouncing his enemies. He toured the state in an expensive limousine with a chauffeur and armed body guards. He was always expensively dressed, often flamboyantly. This required money, and money was something Long never lacked. He was adept at collecting graft and deducted funds from the salaries of state employees.

The law prevented him from running for reelection in 1932, so he ran for United States Senator and won, but did not take his seat in Washington until he put in as governor an old crony, O.K. Allen, who was at his beck and call and under his control. Then he left for Washington, assured of his hold over the state, but spent the majority of time in Louisiana, attending sessions of the legislature and controlling it as a United States Senator by appearing at important committee meetings, calling for votes on the bills he wanted passed and seeing to it that they were.

The Louisiana government was totally dominated by Long; he had become a virtual dictator. His machine remained in power by ruthless political maneuvering and his voting record. The people wanted him; they felt he was God-sent and they came close to worshipping him. They called him the "Kingfish."

Did he fulfill the real needs of the state? What did he do for the little man? In many ways he did, but in an off-balanced fashion. To appease his ego he built elaborate edifices named after him—a state capitol, an airport, the Governor's mansion resembling the White House, athletic facilities, tall office buildings and so forth. On the other hand, he built a highway system, public health facilities, a medical school and night schools to lower the appalling illiteracy rate.

However, he did nothing for tenant farmers and sharecroppers, or to strengthen the labor unions. He was "on the fence" about blacks, insisting publicly that his programs were equally for whites and blacks, yet deep down he nursed a deep-seated animosity. In 1930, as the nation sank into the depression, Louisiana did not have far to go, and it still remains one of the poorest and least developed states in the nation. But Huey Long had other plans.

Long was somewhat of a buffoon, and he learned a technique that captured the attention of the press and thereby national coverage—it was his way of getting to be known. His first venture was to receive a prominent German naval commander dressed in green silk pajamas and a bathrobe. The press was delighted and Huey appeared on the front page of every newspaper in the country!

As he took his seat in the Senate, he proclaimed that his one goal was to spread the wealth among the people. But he was absent more than present, pleading important business of the State of Louisiana. This was a blessing, for when he was present he was a thorn in the sides of the Senators, playing the clown to the hilt, gaining national publicity and inhibiting the orderly proceedings of the Senate.

Then he dropped a bombshell. He discovered that the Senate Democratic leader was a conservative, as were his opponents in Louisiana, and alienated himself from him and the Democratic party by resigning from the committees to which he had been assigned. Once his ties were broken, he launched a diatribe on the Senate floor against the leader, claiming he was profiting from large sums of money from industries that were clients of his law firm in Arkansas. The accusations were false but the adverse publicity went out across the land.

Then Long proceeded to make flamboyant speeches on the need to redistribute the wealth, but did nothing to promote it through legislative channels. He spent only one-third of the time the Senate was in session on the floor, and seemed unconcerned about significant matters when they came up for vote. His flagrant neglect of his duties clearly indicated disinterest and a lack of responsibility. Rather than being destructive, he was more of an irritant to his colleagues, seemed bored and left the hall before the final vote was taken on major bills. He used the Senate for publicity and acclaim, and brushed it aside when topics of greater interest claimed his attention.

The national elections of 1932 were imminent and he concentrated there, and here Huey made his mark. He was an inexhaustible campaigner, and started out to win over the midwestern states for the nomination of Franklin Delano Roosevelt as the Democratic nominee for president. This he did, as well as to gain for himself widespread acclaim. Even James Farley, who ran Roosevelt's campaign, gave him credit, although he was wary of Long and did not trust him.

Then Huey threw himself into the reelection campaign of Hattie Carraway of Arkansas, the widow of Senator Thaddeus Carraway. Hattie was appointed to take his place, and was persuaded by Long to run for the next term. He knew he could mold her into his ways—she had already embraced his plan to redistribute the wealth. He campaigned furiously for her and she won—the first woman in history to sit in the Senate.

The secret of Long's success was winning the confidence and support of the people of the breadbasket of the nation who had suffered years of unemployment and low prices for farm products. They knew he would carry their cause to Washington, and he won the respect of hundreds of thousands who heard him speak as he raced from town to town, drawing them together in his wake. He proclaimed the plight of the little man and vowed to see that amends were made in Washington. Occasionally, voices were raised about electing Long president of the United States in 1936. He was approaching his goal.

Now, Long concentrated on the Senate. He was present every day, reiterating that the voice of the people had been heard and the Democratic leadership must be changed if their will was to be satisfied. Roosevelt was installed as president and his colleagues came to know Huey as an arrogant, aggressive person who was trying to control the Senate as he had the Louisiana legislature—noisy, obstreperous, vituperative. He succeeded repeatedly in slowing down the progress of business and at one point staged a filibuster lasting twenty-one days to prevent the passage of a banking reform bill which he purported obstructed the redistribution of the wealth. It was finally passed, but died in committee when it reached the House too late.

It was apparent that Huey Pierce Long, Jr. was a figure of power; no longer merely an irritant. He had the beginnings of a national following. At this juncture, he introduced a bill on Decentralization of Wealth which he led the people to believe was under the aegis of the Administration. Then he turned his attention to President Roosevelt. Both men, having strong paranoid tendencies, were soon aware that their relationship could never be amicable, however, in order to reach their goals, that they must maintain a semblance of friendship. The great depression was at its lowest and the country rallied behind their new leader. All except Huey. He took issue with every nomination Roosevelt made and made known his opposition to his followers. Every piece of emergency legislation proposed by the White House was objected to by Long in exhaustive speeches in the Senate, with vicious attacks on the proposers. He waged an ongoing battle with Roosevelt.

Many of Roosevelt's appointees came under Long's fire. He deplored the "House of Morgan" and the Rockefellers and accused Wall street of undercutting the little man. His attitude was of total hostility, and he constantly repeated his concept of redistributing the wealth as the only worthwhile method of pulling the country out of the depression. President Roosevelt realized what a dangerous man Long was, and played his hand cagily, as did Long, who aspired to sit in the chair Roosevelt occupied. Their relationship worsened.

Then the President played his hand. He gave federal appointments to Long's opponents in Louisiana. Long countered by instructing the Louisiana government to refuse federal funds that would be under their jurisdiction, and told a press conference that "all the boys in Washington can go to hell!" Roosevelt gambled that his own popularity would offset Long's, and for a while it seemed that he was right. Long was charged with election fraud, which finally proved inconsequential; the Treasury department reopened an investigation into Long's income tax returns, all of which contributed to his embarrassment.

Long's grip was slipping in Louisiana, he no longer drew large crowds, and hostility greeted him as never before. Once he was pelted with eggs. He attacked Roosevelt, and when the heckling was particularly bad, he challenged anyone, surrounded by bodyguards, to come and settle it "man-to-man." His opponents openly carried guns while he spoke.

Then Huey staged a comeback. In the spring of 1934, he shored up his control by ramming through the legislature a group of laws that concentrated his power. He still had the support of the people, and was in total control, even down to local school boards. He was accountable to no one. He forced the Standard Oil Company to accept a tax on oil refined in the state. His opponents were helpless; his enemies were irrational in their hatred.

Long felt secure once again in Louisiana and turned his attention to Washington. He stopped drinking and appearing at bawdy night spots, lost thirty pounds and took his wife with him for the first time. He no longer played the clown and seemed to be responsible and industrious. He concentrated on the redistribution of wealth, and became a frequent speaker on the NBC network. He cited statistics of the Share the Wealth Plan—the Long Plan, he called it—which gave every family the basics: "enough for a home, an automobile, a radio and ordinary conveniences, as a start." In essence, it was "soak the rich and give to the poor". The Plan presented enormous complexities in its execution, but this did not deter Long, even when simple arithmetic made it obvious that there were not enough dollars in the land to finance even the basics.

Huey Long's new image continued in the Senate, where he assumed an active role and took his duties seriously, but used his position to discourse at great length on matters of his own choosing. He used the Senate to exploit his ideas, and the filibuster whenever it suited his purpose. He had no sense of propriety, and made vicious attacks on his colleagues when they tried to obstruct him. He called for an investigation of Postmaster General James A. Farley, one of the President's most loyal and trusted subordinates, claiming graft and corruption in the department. After many months, Long lost, but gained what he was after, publicity and an embarrassed administration. Long earned many enemies among his colleagues; many hated him, some tolerated him, few condoned him.

Early in 1934, Long created a vehicle to install the Plan by establishing the Share Our Wealth Society in every city and town in the country. To counteract this, Roosevelt increased income and inheritances tax rates. Long went along, pressing for more increases. His Share Our Wealth Clubs sprang up across the land. Huey was on his way, already preparing for the 1935 elections, and told reporters "Franklin Roosevelt will not be the next president. If it's Roosevelt and

Hoover, Huey Long will be." He was so sure, he wrote a book entitled "My first days in the White House."

As Roosevelt established programs to pull the nation out of the depression, Long went along in a half-hearted way, always claiming none was sufficient to help the common man—only his Share Our Wealth Plan could do the job. He knew he could not buck the President and his staff of experts, but he could stop the federal programs in Louisiana. It was his boldest stroke yet.

He called the Louisiana legislature into special session, and proposed a series of statutes to block federal funds to the state, in lieu of which he promised to share the wealth. His opponents were up in arms, but in his usual pugnacious manner, and his threats of retribution, he claimed he had to preserve the Constitution of the United States, so his laws were passed by the committee and sent to the House, which was to convene that evening to act upon the bills.

Digress for a moment to meet young Dr. Carl A. Weiss, a successful ear, nose and throat doctor—sensitive, innocuous-looking, married to the daughter of Judge Benjamin Pavy, an anti-Long man, whom Huey was trying to gerrymander off the bench. While not active in politics, Dr. Weiss was highly critical of Long's dictatorship.

The House convened. Because he expected trouble, Huey ordered extra security for his protection—state troopers, plainclothesmen, and examination of all who entered the chamber. The bills passed with scarcely a whimper from the opposition; no federal monies would enter Louisiana.

As Long left the chamber, a young man extended his hand as though to shake Huey's. It held a gun and a shot was fired. Security guards grabbed the gun and shoved Weiss to the floor, pouring thirty-eight bullets into his body. Long staggered, grasping his stomach, and was taken out the back way. Panic ensued as the crowds pressed to escape from the building.

On the way to the hospital, Long's only words were: "I wonder why he shot me." Within the hour it was announced that the assassin was Dr. Carl A. Weiss, unknown to all except his patients. His motives never came to light, the pro-Longs dreamed up their versions; the anti-Longs theirs. Huey Long was dead, and true to his style, left no heir-designate.

Huey Long's paranoia is evident in his life development, beginning as an idealistic yet not unrealistic ambition, developing as he shaped his career, and escalating into the seizure of total power and control through any means—legitimate or not—such as overstepping the bounds of his office. His ego was insatiable; he wouldn't or couldn't listen to the opinions of others. His paranoia culminated in fearful suspicion as he surrounded himself with armed guards. Power and control were his goals.

NERO, MENGISTU, IDI AMIN DADA

We turn now to three political leaders: Nero, who lived in the first century; Mengistu and Idi Amin Dada, who still live as of this writing. They have similar characteristics: cruelty, egocentricity, the overwhelming urge to control and the practice of accusing others for atrocious acts they themselves committed. All are psychopathic paranoid personalities.

Let's look at Nero. Claudius, the fifth Emperor of Rome, married Agrippina after the death of Messelina, who bore him Britannicus and Octavia. He adopted Nero, who, at sixteen, married Octavia. Agrippina conspired to have Nero succeed to the throne over Britannicus after the death of Claudius.

As emperor, Nero had two tutors in Burrus of the Praetorian guards, and the philosopher Seneca, and for a time followed their tutelage, showing promise of a good and sage ruler. Soon, however, paranoia became his dominant passion and he indulged in a life of pleasure and hedonistic pursuits, incurring extraordinary expenses. Added to this, he began to show great cruelty. The first act was the poisoning of Britannicus, the rationale being that Nero had quarreled with his mother, Agrippina, who threatened to depose him and put Britannicus on the throne.

He then proceeded to murder those he suspected of plotting to do away with him. Agrippina was poisoned, then Seneca and Lucan the poet, and his wives, Octavia and Poppaea Sabina. He justified these acts with: "My predecessors did not know the rights of monarchy. People may hate me, but they must also fear me." Apparently, those he destroyed did not. The paranoia was at work.

In A.D. 64, a fire broke out in Rome and burned for nine days. The story goes: "Nero fiddled while Rome burned." He did not care, and had no concern for life or property. But Nero had to blame someone, so he picked on the Christians and persecuted them for setting the fire. Everyone whispered that he had set it, but there was no positive proof. He ordered the Christians thrown to the lions, tortured mercilessly and murdered. The people had come to know too well the cruelty of this man; he was not beyond any dastardly deed of violence.

Then, Nero had the city rebuilt with great extravagance, and for him was erected the "Golden House of Nero." While this was taking place, several groups joined forces to overthrow him, but he caught wind of the conspirators and had them killed. Finally, Galba, a Praetorian guard and the governor of Spain, succeeded in launching a revolution backed by the guards, and the Senate sentenced Nero to death. He was executed in A.D. 68 by the sword of an attendant, at his own request.

Lt. Col. Mengistu Haile Mariam, the totalitarian ruler of Ethiopia, is one of today's extreme paranoid personalities. His ideology is ruining a nation. His dream of making Ethiopia the first African Communist country—a replica of Soviet Russia—so far has come true. He began by manipulating the social structure which culminated in over a million people starving to death. This tragedy was accentuated by a drought, to which the world responded by shipping hundreds of thousands of dollars worth of food to the stricken country. Mengistu saw to it, however, that it did not reach those who needed it and the famine continued.

The long reign of Emperor Haile Selassie was blessed with relative peace, and the country emerged a more modern, better educated nation led by a Western educated group. This exposed the people to the outside world, and demands for freedom and economic reform became widespread, led by student movements in and outside Ethiopia. Minor struggles culminated in the revolution of 1974 and the overthrow of Selassie and his government. People joined one side or the other, some left the country, others were jailed or executed, but none anticipated the events that took place to put the country in the situation it is now in.

Food shortages and famine, civil war and political unrest are the order of the day. Dissidents are imprisoned arbitrarily and tortured. Thousands have disappeared, probably executed without trial. Millions are displaced from their villages and forced to join collective farms. Mengistu is restructuring the social fabric of Ethiopia into a regimented, controlled society. His tools are cruelty and brute force. His efforts have succeeded in making Ethiopia an arm of the Soviet Union, but his dream of turning all of Africa into a totalitarian state will remain unfulfilled as long as there are opposing political systems in Africa and the Middle East.

Mengistu's paranoid frenzy to control and his disregard for human suffering was clearly demonstrated by the way he approached the drought. Seventeen million people were in danger of starving to death, but to him it was merely an aggravation which interfered with his elaborate plans for a four-day celebration to commemorate the tenth year of the revolution which brought him to power. He downplayed the danger and proceeded with the celebration. In the meantime, thousands of Ethiopians were dying and those that could walked to Addis Ababa where he gave orders not to allow them to enter.

The Commission on Relief and Rehabilitation attempted to relocate the people in productive sections of the country, but Mengistu had his own ideas. He wanted to form collective farms run by the government, and forced the people to be herded like cattle into trucks and airplanes and shipped south, out of his way. Millions were saved from starvation by the vast amount of food shipped in from all over the world, but this generosity played into the hand of Mengistu. Without that help there would have been chaos and mass murder resulting in the removal of Mengistu and his regime.

The plight of Ethiopia is fading out of the lime light and no longer attracts the attention of the world. The crisis is over, but there will always be famine and starvation and millions more will die—as long as Mengistu is in control. The Ethiopians need freedom and, if necessary, a revolution to obtain it. Already there are two political groups, the Ethiopian People's Democratic Alliance and the Ethiopian Democratic Union, ready to unite and form a resistance force of thousands of Western-trained military professionals.

From early on, Idi Amin, Dictator of Uganda, demonstrated the influence of witchcraft with which his environment was permeated, and was mildly manifest in the "cargo" cults. Here is a man whose cruel, psychopathic tendencies were apparent early in life, but only mental derangement can explain his excessive actions. Here is his story.

Uganda gained its independence from the United Kingdom in 1963. It is a country rife with tribalism and witchcraft; mysticism and brutal rites have been the order of the land. Although many Ugandans have become Christians, they still cling to the superstitious remnants of witchcraft.

Idi Amin Dada was born about 1927; his father came from the Kakwa tribe, his mother was versed in witchcraft. She knew how to prepare the "Lion's Water," also called Yakan and Allah's Water, which produced elation, excitement and a sense of frenzy when taken to excess, and was used before going into battle to ward off bullets. It came from a plant of the daffodil family that grew in the Kakwa country and the source of a drug that produces illusions and visions. It was the LSD of central Africa.

Idi's birth was long and difficult; he weighed twelve pounds. While still a baby, his mother ran away to live with her tribesmen, so his childhood was rootless. He grew up with witchcraft and punishments, incantations and rites to the spirits called upon by his mother. He was a large boy and used his size to control his peers. He overcame his opponents by crushing their genitals in his huge fists. The potential of paranoia showed up early in life. At sixteen, Idi, steeped in witchcraft, became a Muslim, but did he know the implications? An African who became a Muslim was called a Nubi in the army and considered cannon fodder for the British.

When independence approached, the British moved fast to prepare for African leadership, and Amin was sent to a crash course in officer training. He was ambitious and, regardless of his lack of education, intelligent enough to know that his climb up would be frustrating and slow. He was six feet four and strong—a good athlete, and heavyweight boxing champion of the army. His trainer was worried about his attitude when he entered the ring—not to win, but to kill. His paranoia was showing, but he was obedient, took orders well, showing a desire to please, and was subservient as befitted his position. He was building up his image. Soon, Idi was promoted to corporal.

Idi Amin could speak little English, but showed outstanding signs of leadership and was well liked. While he worked his way up to the rank of officer, he displayed a keen competitive sense. It was incumbent upon British officers to promote Africans, so Idi Amin was commissioned a warrant officer. Now his paranoia erupted in an unpleasant form. When interrogating prisoners, he forced them to confess by commanding them to place their penises on a table, while he stood by with a machete. The responses were quick.

In the rush to independence, more authority was meted out, and in Amin's case, the more he had, the more his cruelty was revealed. As he rose to power, he was responsible for several reprehensible acts which deserved severe disciplinary measures, but none was taken. This added to his sense of power. He was now a major in command of a company and his modus operandi was to carry out his orders, then slaughter, maim or torture his captives. In one operation, he was known to have chopped off the penises of eight men who did not reply to his questions quickly enough. These atrocities were performed in Kenya and complaints were sent to the Kenyan government. The British were shocked, but could do nothing. Governor Sir Walter Coutts apprised Milton Obote, the prime minister-designate, with "I warn you that this officer will cause trouble in the future." But criminal proceedings would have had serious repercussions at that time. Now Uganda was independent, and Idi lost no time insinuating himself into the good graces of the ruling politicians. His uncle, Felix Onoma, was Minister of the Interior, and soon after independence, Prime Minister Obote went to Israel, taking Amin with him as an aide-de-camp. A year later he was made a Colonel and moved closer to the inner circle of government.

Now Obote was president and nationalized British interests in Uganda—banking, tea, coffee. Idi Amin was quickly advanced to Brigadier and then General, and with this new authority, was able to build a formidable following among his Nubian and Kakwa blood-brothers. At this juncture, Obote and Amin were suspected of smuggling gold and ivory from the Congo. Both their bank accounts had received large amounts of money.

In 1969, an attempt was made to assassinate Obote. When Idi Amin was alerted, he ran out the back door of his house and went into hiding; sentiment ran high against him. His severest critic was Brigadier Okoya, and the next day the Brigadier and his wife were found murdered in their home. Evidence pointed toward Amin. During the next year the climate between Obote and Amin became more antagonistic, as Amin wormed his way into Obote's inner circle of influential advisors. The politics in Africa were extremely involved, further complicated by the different religious groups, especially the Muslims and Christians.

Obote had many problems and his difficulties with Amin escalated. Amin kept building his corps of officers from tribes of the region where he was born, and ignored those from Obote's tribe, thus building a base loyal only to him. These policies were pointed out to Obote, as well as evidence that over two million pounds were missing from the army funds which were controlled by Amin.

At midnight in January 1971, Idi Amin Dada staged his coup. Obote was attending the Commonwealth Conference in Singapore, and his assassination was planned at the airport in Kenya on his return. It was aborted, but non-the-less Amin took over power. There was no bloodshed, and Obote was whisked to a hotel. Amin quickly organized an administration. He was totally a military man and ignored the needs of his countrymen other than military. He transformed the Defense Council into a one-man council—he as Commander in Chief, Army Chief of Staff, Air Chief of Staff, with the power to appoint others, but none were ever appointed except his cronies. His paranoia was directing him and he mounted a series of massacres against the tribes most likely to be loyal to Obote.

Unfortunately, Great Britain speedily recognized Amin's regime. He shopped around for defense contracts with Britain and offensive weapons with Israel. He met with Abba Eban, the foreign minister and General Mosha Dayan of Israel about free port facilities for his landlocked country. If he didn't get them, he would take them by force, but the Ugandans were friendly with the Israelis, for at one time Uganda was considered a location for the homeland of the Jews.

Amin believed his economic problems could be solved if oil were discovered in Uganda. Although Shell Oil had already concluded that the potential was not cost effective, Amin found a British company eager to try; a limited amount was found and he contracted with the company to go ahead. Previously, he had met Gadaffi of Libya and established cordial relationships, so he discussed the oil project with him. Gadaffi talked him out of it as too risky, and persuaded him to form ties with the Arabs and sever connections with Britain and Israel, claiming they would never provide sufficient military equipment. Always irrational, Idi went along and in one move abandoned Britain, Europe, Israel and the Asians and clung only to Libya.

By now Amin had brought his country deeper into economic distress, and figured that through the wealthy Muslim countries he could get what he wanted. An announcement was made by Amin and Gadaffi that Uganda was the ally of the Arabs and the Palestinians. Now Amin planned to "eliminate the few remaining Christians and turn Uganda into a Muslin state." At this time Uganda was six percent Muslim, the rest Christian.

To accomplish his goals, at a meeting of the Cabinet of the Second Republic of Uganda, Amin proposed and it was made into law that any minister who felt his life was threatened had the right to kill in self defense. Thus, Amin had a legal way of disposing of his enemies, and put everyone on the alert, for the slightest ripple of trouble ended in the killing of those whom Amin designated as his opponents.

In March, 1972, all Israeli and Asian personnel holding British passports were ordered to leave Uganda. This marked the decline that broke Uganda's back, for the Asians had a powerful grip on the economy and had not trained the Africans in entrepreneurship, but held them back doing menial work. The system of supply and demand soon evolved into chaos, black markets developed, and shortages of important staples were causing great hardship.

In September of 1972, Obote's forces tried to overthrow Amin, but were repulsed by soldiers flown in from Libya. Edward Rugumayo, Amin's minister of Education, defected in 1973 and urged the Organization for African Unity, the United Nations and the Commonwealth to condemn him. He describes Amin as an illiterate soldier of low intelligence, who cannot read or write and speaks poor English and is medically unfit, suffering from a hormone defect. He is a racist, a tribalist and a dictator with no principles, moral standards or scruples; he will kill or cause to have killed anyone as long as it serves his purpose. He is an incorrigible liar, unreliable and unpredictable.

He has a Jekyll-and-Hyde character. His dynamic personality greatly impresses those he met for the first time. He can be gentle, charming and generous in order to win the good graces of someone who might be valuable to him. He seems incapable of wrong-doing or of hurting someone, and has the capacity to be friendly and warm one moment and switch to brutality and murder the next. He is a master manipulator and kills coolly and rationally; he enjoys inviting for drinks those he is about to have murdered. As Amin grew older, he was subject to ungovernable outbursts of temper. On one occasion, he confessed: "I lost my temper; I killed him."

Amin was highly suspicious of intellectuals and anyone who had a higher degree of knowledge or experience. Then he fell back on his belief in magic to bolster his self-esteem and proclaim that he is all-powerful and God has ordained that he cannot be harmed. He was certain that his ideas were superior to all others; and gave orders verbally and expected reports that they had been followed. Usually, they were to murder an individual; the code was "Give him the VIP treatment," which meant to torture, then kill. His staff feared for their lives if they disobeyed.

Amin was unable to analyze situations, and although warned by his ministers, they were wrong, he was right—paranoia. He ruled Uganda by magic, dreams and witchcraft, and what they revealed to him. Medicine men were consulted and their instructions carried out in detail. One ordained that Amin eat the heart of his most loved son, and he did, after killing him.

With power at his command, Idi Amin surrounded himself with tight security; he was suspicious of everyone. The management of the moneys was loose as there were no reports, no records and soon it was clear that funds were short. Amin and his friends, however, were well supplied. Idi's paranoia was busy at work—a military junta was in command and the cruelty was unbelievable. The police killed innocent people as they walked along the street; public executions were staged; some prisoners were tortured, then executed, sometimes by a blow to the head with a sledge hammer—it was less expensive than using bullets! The people watched in horror. It is estimated that Amin slaughtered ten thousand Ugandans a week; what their crimes were was never divulged.

Amin governed by brute force; it was the only method he knew. He ordered the torture and murder of persons whose wealth he coveted or whose intellectuality he was envious of. He had no concern for the suffering he imposed, nor loyalty for a person once his usefulness to him was over. His wives did not escape, nor did his children. He cooly described in detail on television the dismembered body of his wife whom he had murdered. His lust for power was enormous and he kept his ministers and generals on tenterhooks; they never knew who would be next. Thus he kept power and control. Idi Amin was deeply insecure; high paranoia trusts no one and suspicion and hostility fed on his low intelligence. Having no scruples, he wove web after web of lies, which if questioned, resulted in the murder of the person involved. The makeup of the army had changed, as brought about by Amin. Its members were ruthless men with no regard for human life, and no loyalty to Uganda, for they were Libyans, Palestinians and Nubians. Another of many attempts on Amin's life took place but was aborted by chance. Amin responded with ravaging purges of the army.

The killings continued; the devastation was beyond belief, as was the torment and despair of the Ugandan people, unaware of why these savage beatings and brutality took place. The surrounding African nations were also plundered and destroyed, villages pillaged and burned, if Amin had the slightest hint that they were plotting to do him in.

By the end of 1977, Amin's genocide continued to gain momentum. The methods of killing became more vicious, barbaric and brutal.

The torture is too inhuman to recount, the suffering unbearable. While this went on, Amin ordered expensive medals from England made by its finest jewelers—all for himself. And why didn't the United Nations step in? Based on the principle that external governments cannot interfere in the domestic affairs of other nations, member nations claim immunity. So Amin was allowed to continue his bloodbath for almost eight years. It is a sad commentary that the international community was helpless to stop the carnage of a fellow nation.

In the spring of 1978, cracks appeared in Amin's command. He had a falling out with some of his ministers and several of his top people defected. Many of his soldiers drifted over the border to Tanzania, where they waited for his downfall. Amin called on Gadaffi for assistance, claiming that Tanzania was invading Uganda—a total lie. The Ugandan National Liberation Front was formed there under Colonels Ikello and Ojok, and as the news got out, thousands of Ugandans gathered under them from all parts of the world where they had gone into exile. Gadaffi sent Libyans, but they were no match for the liberation army, and Amin and his troops retreated northward, looting, stealing and killing all in their path. The liberation army went after them and annihilated them. And where was Idi Amin Dada? He had vanished, conquered at last. Where is he now? Is he still alive?

The latest news in 1989 about Idi Amin Dada is scant. Since being thrown out of Uganda in 1979, he and his family have lived in Saudi Arabia. He was granted exile there on the condition he refrain from political activity, but he persisted in contacting individuals in an effort to return to power in Uganda. Recently, he went back to Africa after a dispute with the Saudi government, and reportedly flew out of Zaire in January, his destination Saudi Arabia, but there is no report of his arrival. His family remains there.

We have given examples of paranoid personalities you meet in the course of a lifetime who are relatively harmless. Then we described types who have wide spheres of influence and can be called benign, such as John Noyes, John Pierpont Morgan, John Edgar Hoover and John Patterson. We have gradually increased the paranoid intensity of the characters such as Indira Gandhi and Aimee Semple McPherson, which brings us to two of the most destructive types—Josef Stalin and Adolf Hitler. Both these men succeeded in terrorizing the world and eliminating millions of innocent people. Their actions changed the course of history, and influenced immeasurably the lives of millions. Here are their stories in brief.

JOSEF STALIN

Josef Stalin was born in Gori, Georgia in 1879. His parents were freed Georgian serfs, his father a mediocre shoemaker, his mother a washerwoman. In his learning years, he was a rebellious, dictatorial and questioning child. His excessive paranoia was apparent from early childhood.

He attended the Orthodox parochial school, proved a brilliant student and was awarded a scholarship to be trained for the priesthood. At the seminary, he joined a hot-bed of student radicals who were protesting the Czar's rule over Georgians as a minority race. This and the harsh, monastic regime of the seminary propelled him into Marxism, for which subversive views he was expelled.

At twenty, he secured a job as a clerk, and moonlighted as a Marxist agitator, until his job was terminated by the police. From then on he devoted himself to underground political activities and edited a Marxist newspaper. He was arrested, spent two years in prison and was exiled to Siberia from where he escaped.

At twenty-six, he joined Lenin, who had split the workers' party into the Bolsheviks and the Mensheviks. Stalin joined the more militant Bolsheviks, returned to the Caucasus and headed the fighting squads, conducting robberies to finance their activities. During the next five years, he was arrested, exiled and escaped three times. In 1912, Stalin was appointed by Lenin to the Central Committee of the Bolshevik Party. He founded the newspaper Pravda and became its first editor. A year later he was again arrested and exiled to Siberia, but did not try to escape. In 1916, he was declared unfit for military duty in World War I because of his withered left arm—a holdover from a serious infection in childhood.

When the Czar abdicated in 1917, Stalin was released from exile and elected a member of the Bolshevik party's first Politburo, and when they seized power during the revolution, Stalin was one of the leaders. He climbed to one high position after another until he was made secretary general of the USSR Communist Party in 1922, and quickly gained control of the entire party apparatus.

When Lenin died in 1924, Stalin was virtually the ruler of the Soviet Union despite opposition from the dying Lenin and strong competition from Politburo members. As each opposed his policies, he removed them one by one from the Politburo. Trotsky, Stalin's greatest rival, was exiled to Central Asia and then deported. Now Stalin was in total control. His paranoia had succeeded.

From then on Stalin ruled Russia. He changed the economy from Lenin's policies to the five-year plans. Private enterprise was nationalized or turned into state-controlled cooperatives. Peasants were forced to work on huge mechanized farms, and in record time, industry concentrated on heavy rather than light manufacturing, neglecting housing and consumer goods. All resistance was crushed by increasingly intensified dictatorship. Prison labor camps sprang up; art and education produced only Stalinist propaganda. Stalin's second wife, one of Lenin's former secretaries, died under mysterious circumstances. His control deepened and widened.

From 1934 to 1938, Stalin conducted his great internal purge, eradicating by demotion, prison or execution most of the cabinet and legislative officials, including the majority of central committeemen and army officers. His suspicion conceived a conspiracy which he alleged was devised by those he eliminated. He exerted his authority into the core of society by ordering hero-worship of himself to dominate the arts, the schools, and the press. On the eve of the Soviet-German war, he appointed himself premier, head of the State Defense Committee (the war cabinet) and generalissimo—the highest military office in the USSR.

After the war, he resigned the military leadership, retaining the premiership and rank of generalissimo, and withdrew into semiretirement because of heart disease. He devoted his time to writing and published instructions to Soviet writers on political economy. His last public speech in 1952 supported foreign Communist parties in their attempts to seize power and included the subsidization of heavy industry and armament for years to come. He insisted that the economy ignore consumer needs, expand a war-potential industry and exert tighter control by the state over all cooperatives. Stalin died in 1953, and his paranoid ideology is still felt in Russia.

ADOLF HITLER

Adolf Hitler was born April 20, 1889 in Linz, Austria, the fifth of Alois and Klara Hitler's seven children. At an early age he showed strong paranoid tendencies by displaying a lack of obedience and vehemently quarreling with his father. In German households the father is the authoritative figure, but Adolf defied his.

Adolf did fairly well at school. He loved to make speeches and irritated his playmates by preaching to them. He wanted to be important, to expand his image. His compulsion to control was paramount, so his destiny was evident from early childhood. In sixth grade, his marks began to fail and he blamed his father and his teachers. At sixteen he dropped out.

Adolf would not accept authority from any source, and had an over-inflated ego and a strong sense of self-importance. He was always right and his ideas were better than anyone's. When things didn't work out, his failure was someone else's fault.

His father died and his mother had him apprenticed to a paper hanger, but he soon left and lived on her small pension. Although he professed love for her, he felt no shame at sharing her meagre income, never thinking that she might be deprived. He always wanted to be an artist, and for the next three years he loafed, dreaming of his future as an artist. He spent the evenings at the opera, or read books on history. He thought a lot and brooded about the state of the world. He was a pale, sickly youth, usually shy and reticent, but would fly into a rage if someone crossed him. Already taking shape was a strong paranoid personality.

At eighteen, Hitler went to the Vienna Academy of Fine Arts, but his test drawings were below standard and he was not admitted. He resented this and developed an intense hatred of Vienna and all things Austro-Hungarian. His distorted logic blamed his love of Germany and "stupid" teachers for the rejection by the Academy, not his lack of talent.

The following year his mother died of cancer. He faced a dilemma; he had never worked and was suddenly aware he had to make a living. He took off for Vienna but shunned a regular job, preferring to shovel snow, and beat carpets, but only long enough to buy food. He lived in flophouses, was dirty and unshaven—a bum. And he was miserable.

He claimed that those years taught him all he knew about life. He came to glorify war, and felt that the maiming of men and the loss of young lives was irrelevant to the purpose. But how did he shape the plan he subsequently carried out? He learned about politics, and that its power is to attract millions by distorting truth, which is believed if presented to the public in the proper manner. Politics also means using threats and terror, even killing in order to gain control under all circumstances. And Hitler learned that oratory sways the masses and became the greatest orator of his time—only Winston Churchill was his equal.

It was in Vienna that he conceived his hatred of Jews, which became mad fanaticism. He moved to Munich and was happy there, for he loved Germany and considered Germans the Master Race. He had visions of making good in the world—but how he didn't know.

In 1914, the first World War began and Hitler joined a Bavarian regiment. He served four years as a dispatch runner but never rose above corporal, and claimed to have been wounded and decorated twice with the Iron Cross. On November 10, 1918, the news came that the British had won the war, and Hitler sobbed. Soon after, he decided to go into politics. It was a fateful decision for the world.

His prospects were bleak; he was nameless, moneyless, jobless, with little schooling, and no experience, but Hitler had enormous confidence and was sure the opportunity would come—and it did. He joined a group to educate civilians in militarism. The members were assigned to infiltrate under cover and report on political groups, and Hitler was sent to the "German Workers' Party," from which he molded the Nazi party. He was a brilliant organizer and shrewd propagandist; his message was that Germany had not lost the war but was stabbed in the back by the Jews, socialists and communists. His speeches were long, and he spoke in a rough dialect with poor grammar. Nonetheless, his frenzy was transmitted to his audiences.

He went about inciting crowds with his oratory, so much so that he asked for bodyguards; they were brown-shirted toughs who terrorized Hitler's opponents, broke up their meetings, beat them and if necessary, killed them. They became the SA storm troopers. Hitler changed the name of the party to the National Socialist German Workers' Party, from which is derived the term "Nazi," from Nationalsozialistsche. He called himself the Fuehrer—leader. He was at the top, above everyone. Among those who followed him were characters such as Goebbels, Goering, Himmler, Hess and Roehm—misfits all, who added their clout to his. This blend resulted in a destructive force unequalled in world history. He attracted strong as well as weak, but both carried out his orders of annihilation.

First, Hitler attempted to take over the government via the Beer Hall Putsch. Germany was in a mess politically and socially, and the people looked for someone, anyone who promised better times. On November 8, 1923, Hitler led the storm troopers to take over a beer hall where a political rally was taking place and he would persuade the leaders to join his revolution. The government was alerted, however, and sent the army. Hitler's group was destroyed, the party disbanded and the leaders tried for high treason. Hitler dominated the courtroom with his eloquence, establishing himself as a national figure. Nonetheless, he was found guilty and sentenced to five years in prison where he wrote the book "Mein Kampf," "My Struggle." It eventually outsold all books except the Bible and made Hitler a millionaire.

Hitler wanted Germany to become master of the world. He planned to tear up the Versaille Treaty, destroy France, then Austria, Czechoslovakia, Poland and Russia. He would be dictator of Germany and her conquests, and next, he will settle with the Jews. His paranoia was running him.

In 1929, the Wall Street crash resulted in worldwide depression, and this gave Hitler his chance. There was hunger, chaos, confusion, despair. Banks failed, jobs were lost, businesses went under. Hitler promised the people a way out; he would have jobs for them, put business back on its feet, and open the banks. He was euphoric, and at this point indulged himself in luxury and extravagance. If his demands were not met, he ranted and raved until they were. His temperament was volatile—he wept if something went wrong and suffered from extreme inertia or frantic activity.

The Nazi Party lost seats in the Reichstag in the next two elections. The majority of Germans still rejected Hitler, who used his power of manipulation to purge the party of his enemies and win over

President von Hindenburg. With the help of Franz von Papen, he worked out a deal with the aging president to make him chancellor and von Papen vice-chancellor. Hitler now headed the republic he had sworn to destroy, and a year and a half later he was dictator of Germany. Completely in command, he showed his true personality— a bloodthirsty, unscrupulous tyrant, who stopped at nothing to gain his ends. Yet, the majority of the people revered him.

Von Papen, was a non-Nazi conservative and considered Hitler's rise to power a token gesture. He was wrong. Within eighteen months Papen and his colleagues were eliminated; every party except the Nazi was outlawed as well as all democratic and republican institutions. Germany was totally Nazified. Hitler abolished freedom of speech, denied the people civil rights, persecuted the Christian churches and hounded the Jews. He ordered many murdered and others taken to concentration camps where they were beaten or killed. This was aggressive, ruthless control.

Hitler aspired to succeed Hindenburg, who was old and failing in health, so he made another deal with the generals to make him president, and he began what is known as the Nazi Blood Purge. Over one thousand persons were murdered on his orders during one weekend, including leaders of the SA and others he distrusted, also Ernst Roehm, his closest friend.

A few weeks later, Hindenburg died; Hitler maneuvered to succeed him, combined the offices of president and chancellor,, and made himself Commander-in-Chief of the Armed Forces. Now, his way was clear to conquer Europe and become "Master of the World." He re-armed Germany in defiance of the Versailles Treaty—army, air force and navy. In November 1937, he announced that he was going to war; his first campaign will be bloodless, he will conquer by diplomacy, threat and deception.

First, Hitler called the Austrian chancellor to Berchtesgaden and threatened to crush Austria unless he surrendered. He shouted and stormed, demanding that the chancellor sign the agreement, and he did. Nevertheless, Hitler marched with his army into Austria and threw the chancellor into jail. His next victim was Czechoslovakia. Neville Chamberlain, Prime Minister of Great Britain, and Premier Daladier of France were at his side, and persuaded the Czechs to surrender Czechoslovakia by threatening the destruction of Prague by air unless the president signed—he did.

Poland was next. Hitler lined up Italy as an ally and ordered the German army to march in, even though he was not sure of Russia. Next he planned war with France and Britain. Belgium and Holland were easy and would give him a position to take France. Then he could attack Britain by air.

First he had to win Russia over, but found that Stalin was his match—unscrupulous, evil, double-dealing and paranoid, who was also negotiating with Britain and France, but agreed to stay out of any war in which Germany was engaged. Secretly, the two dictators made a pact to divide Poland, and Russia to annex Latvia, Estonia and Finland. Eventually, this was done.

Mussolini reneged on his treaty to help Hitler take Poland. Now Hitler wanted war, and worked himself into a diabolical, hysterical frenzy and launched World War II. At 4:30 a.m. on September 1, 1939, the German army poured across the Polish borders and bombers flew over in waves dropping destruction. German submarines waited in the waters around Britain. When Germany did not withdraw from Poland, the British and French declared war.

For the next three years, Adolf Hitler was victorious beyond his wildest dreams. Even his generals recognized the tyrant that he was— a dangerous, irresponsible megalomaniac. Yet he proved to be a military genius, and often went over their heads. In 1940, Denmark and Norway were occupied, the German army marched across the borders of Holland and Belgium and on into France. Within six weeks, all had surrendered. Now they were at the English channel, and Hitler could take his revenge for the loss of World War I.

Hitler was elated and dizzy with success. He had most of Europe; only Britain was left and he could easily take her. But he didn't understand naval warfare, and personally was afraid of water. Italy had joined Hitler and needed his help against the British in the Mediterranean, but he would have none of this. Instead, he went after his ally, the Soviet Union. No conqueror had ever taken Russia—not Charles of Sweden nor Hitler's idol, Napoleon. But he believed that he could, regardless of the Russian winter which had frustrated Napoleon. His judgment was faulty, however, fed by his compulsion to control.

In December 1941, the Japanese bombed Pearl Harbor, bringing the United States into the war. This was Hitler's chance to capture another powerful nation. He joined the Japanese and declared war on the United States! His paranoia was sparked, and the flames were fanned, driving him on to more and more foolishness. The German armies nearly perished that winter but Hitler refused to allow them to retreat. His generals disagreed, so he fired one after the other and took over as commander-in-chief.

When summer came, he resumed the offensive and General Rommel drove the British back in Africa. His submarines sank allied ships at the rate of 700,000 tons a month. But in Russia, he tried to control a larger front than was possible and his chief of staff recommended that they pull back. Hitler flew into a rage, dismissed the general and threw another tantrum—it was the beginning of his downfall.

Hitler seemed to have lost touch with reality. Although his mind was disintegrating, his fierce will kept him going. The German armies were surrounded by Russians, and his generals begged him to let them fight their way out, but he refused. The wounded were dying for lack of care and the army was starving for lack of supplies, but Hitler gave orders to hold out. He said he preferred that the last man be slaughtered rather than surrender.

Finally, Paulus, the general in command, went against Hitler's orders and surrendered. Hitler, safe in his heated headquarters, raved and ranted. It was February, twenty-four below zero and the 91,000 German soldiers, many wounded, were forced to walk to Siberia and the detention camps. He had no sympathy for the 100,000 Germans slaughtered in Stalingrad, nor the suffering of the prisoners. He was disintegrating mentally and physically; he took drugs to sleep and to stop shaking. He was without reason and never admitted the folly of his judgment. All seemed lost, but he managed to hold out for two more bloody years!

Now the mad dictator ordained the "New Order": that the Nazis would rule Europe, and the peoples they captured would be the slaves of the "Master Race." First the Jews and many of the Slavs would be exterminated. The horrors began. Although many shied at carrying out these orders, if one balked, he was shot. Seven and a half million civilians—men, women. and children—were forced to work at slave labor in Germany, half starved, housed in hovels. Millions more were placed in concentration camps where most died or were put to death. Of Europe's ten million Jews, nearly five million were massacred in gas chambers; another three-quarters of a million shot to death. Hitler took pleasure in boasting of "wiping all Jews off the face of the earth." When one of his top men was assassinated, he took revenge by killing over a thousand Czechs.

By this time, the Anglo-American armies had landed on the beaches of Normandy and were marching to Paris. Mussolini was overthrown, so Hitler commanded the German troops in Italy to seize the royal family and the generals and destroy them. In July 1944, an attempt was made to kill Hitler, however, because one of the generals inadvertently moved the brief case containing the time bomb, Hitler was only slightly injured. Then he went into a violent rage. His revenge was to torture and put to death those responsible, their wives and children, and thousands of suspects, both military and civilian, including most of his generals.

Hitler was visibly deteriorating in body and mind. He was cruel, deceitful, told lie after lie, trusted nobody, yet succeeded in rallying the German armies to prolong the war for another year.

In August 1944, the German generals concluded the war was over, but not Hitler. He scraped up what was left of his army and staged an offensive against the American front known as the Battle of the Bulge, and on Christmas Day the Americans won. Then the Russians struck from the East and marched on toward Berlin.

Soon, Hitler realized all was lost and, typically paranoid, placed the blame on others. He went out of control and pulled a tantrum of deadly proportions. Then he gave his last order: destroy all areas threatened by the Russian and Anglo-American armies. That meant Germans and captives, he wanted all annihilated—men, women and children. If he had to go, everyone had to go. Some officers and generals refused. The allies reached Berlin on April 21, 1945.

Hitler was doomed at last. He summoned Eva Braun, his friend for thirteen years, to share his fifty-sixth birthday. He was still confident he could win and ordered an all-out attack on the advancing Russians, and if forces are held back the commander will be executed. There was no attack.

When Hitler heard the Russians were in Berlin, he staged the greatest rage of his life. As they neared his underground headquarters, he calmed down and planned his last days. He married Eva Braun, wrote his will and directed how he and his bride would die. In his will, he blamed the Jews for the ills of mankind, for provoking the war and for the millions of deaths in battle, the concentration camps and gas chambers! When the Russians were a block away, he shot himself. Eva Braun took poison. The bodies were covered with gasoline in a shell hole and burned. No traces were found. Another version is that he took cyanide, then Eva shot him and took cyanide herself. It was April 30, 1945.

The world knows Hitler for his insatiable greed for power, his ruthlessness, his cruelty, his lack of moral restraint and total disregard for human life and suffering. No man in history has been linked with more major crimes. Totally absent in his makeup were the traits of decency, honesty, gratitude, justice, kindness, love. Yet he had a strange hold over his followers, and a charisma that captivated thousands. How can this be explained? Was he spawned by Satan? When his plans went well, he was insanely euphoric; when they went awry he flared up into a madman's rage and blamed the Jews, the French, the English, the Americans. His paranoia caught fire and spread into national paranoia, and the country believed in him! Thus, he was able to exert control over countless numbers of people, and to gather around him individuals who stood by him and obeyed his brutally sadistic orders.

All who crossed Hitler were doomed. The young men of that time had no course but to join the Nazi party or be killed. The death camps were filled with all kinds of people, not only Jews, and he murdered Gypsies, the mentally retarded, defectives and so forth. And when he was losing, he exterminated everyone, Germans included.

In direct contrast to this fanatically destructive paranoid type was Winston Spencer Churchill, a benign dictator.

WINSTON SPENCER CHURCHILL

On the 30th of November 1874, Winston Spencer Churchill was born to Lord and Lady Randolph Churchill. His mother was Jeannette Jerome, an American. He was brought up in Victorian England when the children of a certain stratum of society were attended to by a "nannie". At specified hours they were washed, dressed and combed and presented to their parents for a short time, then whisked away. All his life, Winston bemoaned the fact that he never knew his parents.

Lord Randolph, a brilliant man, considered his son of below average intelligence and chose for him the military as a career, much to Winston's delight. He worshipped his father, and when Lord Randolph died at the age of forty-six, he grieved the loss of a father he never really knew.

Winston was blue-eyed, freckled and red-haired and, as a small boy, pig-headed, rebellious and mischievous. He went through an array of nursemaids and ended up with a nannie, Mrs. Everest, to whom he became greatly attached and regarded her his best friend. He was sent to Harrow where his marks were poor; he was argumentative, and refused to learn Latin, which subjected him to frequent "canings." He was the school clown and always on the edge of being expelled; all he learned at Harrow was to write the English language properly

High paranoia was already discernible in Winston. He was truculent, unmanageable and wanted his way. He refused to conform and was averse to being taught, which put him at the bottom of his class in every school he attended. In his mind, he knew best and the opinion of grown-ups was invalid. This quality prevailed through his entire life.

Although his scholastic record was dismal, the experience gave him an insatiable urge to do better and to never give in. He went to Sandhurst where he joined the cavalry, played polo and engaged in the hunt, which he greatly enjoyed. He was avid for knowledge and had a love for words, but did not know their precise meaning or how to use them, so he embarked on a course of reading.

Always thirsting for action, Winston applied for a commission to India where war had broken out. He was made war correspondent for the Allahabad Pioneer. He wrote his first book which was widely acclaimed and the compliments filled him with pride. He loved to write and made a momentous decision—writing would be his livelihood. To him "writing was great fun" and his ability was enhanced as he discovered he could color his writing with his artistic flair.

The Army paid Winston a bare subsistence, so he submitted his resignation as his writings had earned enough to support him for two years. One day he noticed a sign "Speakers Wanted" in a store window. Speaking had never occurred to him and he jumped at the opportunity to test his skill. Ten days later his political speech, which he had memorized, was received with high approval. Thus he embarked on another career and became the greatest orator of modern history.

The Boer War was brewing and Churchill went to South Africa as a war correspondent for the morning Post. He dwelled on the fact that his father died young and he probably would also, so he had to accomplish what he set out to do before the age of forty. He was labeled the "impetuous young man on the run." In addition, he had an incredible memory, an ability to retain facts and an enormous amount of energy. Always stimulated by excitement, he joined the soldiers in an attack by the Boers, was captured and put in prison but soon escaped. Inspired by the exhilaration, he rejoined the Army as a lieutenant and, when the war was won in 1902, returned to England to seek public office.

He campaigned over a grueling six weeks, was elected and won a seat for his party. His speeches were loudly applauded and he received congratulations from the Prime Minister and others in high office. Parliament was to meet in December when he would make his debut, so he buckled down to concentrate on politics. He realized he must forgo his writing for the time being, so made a lecture tour of the United States and Canada to supplement his income and was well received. He was twenty-six.

Churchill entered the House of Commons and took his father's seat. It was the custom for a new member to wait for a few sessions before speaking, but not Winston. He was fully prepared, his speech memorized and he chose as his subject, South Africa. At the end he was applauded and congratulated and thus began his distinguished career.

Winston was an indifferent extemporaneous speaker. He had a slight lisp and avoided as much as possible words ending in "s," so he memorized every speech. His sense of humor was rich with witticisms and he seldom missed a chance to cast a barb at a member of the House who might have blundered. He was never embarrassed or self-conscious, but often infuriated his audience with his caustic remarks about his opponents. He showed a flair for eulogizing his contemporaries, referring to Sir Stafford Cripps, for whom he had a pet aversion, as Sir Stifford Crapps; he called Ramsay MacDonald "a boneless wonder," Hitler, a "bloodthirsty guttersnipe" and Mussolini, "a whipped jackal." In regard to forming policy, he once said: "We will operate on

the Italian donkey at both ends—with a carrot and with a stick".
Although a Conservative, Churchill leaned toward the Liberal
Party. This lost him the backing of the Conservatives. Then came his
break with the Party, which was slowly disintegrating, when he was
wooed by the Liberals of Manchester and accepted. Shortly afterward,
he left his seat on the Conservative side and chose the Liberal side,
which was propitious for him and the Party. Although he won, he ran
up against a formidable foe—the suffragettes. They harassed him,
disrupted his meetings and interrupted his speeches.

Winston made many friends and one of the most valued was
Lord Hugh Cecil to whom he was drawn by a rare and individual
mind. He was also popular with the people as he addressed the
problems of the poor and fought for the alleviation of poverty. They
also loved his propensity for unusual hats and dress, his enthusiasm,
his droll sense of humor. In his election address in January 1906,
Churchill pledged free trade, religious equality, reduction of expendi-
ture on arms and control of education. Soon he was asked by Prime
Minister Chamberlain to guide the new constitution of South Africa
through the House of Commons, which he did with skill.

Winston had long aspired to be a member of the Cabinet and at
last was offered the position as head of the Board of Trade; he
considered himself a social reformer and felt his best chance was in this
role. Another member was Lloyd George whom Winston came to
respect and admire. Lloyd George grew up in poverty, Winston within
the privileged class, so he had much to learn from his colleague whose
leadership was the only one he ever accepted. Churchill did ground-
breaking work at the Board of Trade. He exposed the scandals of the
sweatshops, people working in appalling conditions for long hours
and low pay. He had passed the Trade Board's Act, then went after the
problem of unemployment, and instituted labor exchanges and unemployment insurance.

A rift developed in the accord within the Cabinet over the
number of dreadnoughts to be built because of imminent trouble
between Austria and Germany. Churchill insisted that fewer ships
would suffice. This shook the confidence of his friends, that he should
downgrade the importance of the Navy in favor of social issues.
Winston, in all his assignments was possessed by his own opinions and
seldom listened to what others had to say, wholly obsessed by his
determination to have his views heard. His paranoia was apparent.

Discussions over the budget lasted seven months, often breaking
into raging arguments. Lloyd George berated the dukes, claiming it
takes as much money to support one as to maintain two dreadnoughts.
Churchill joined in vilifying the peerage and was accused of betraying
his heritage. Thus arose a schism so serious between the House of
Lords and the House of Commons that King Edward summoned

Prime Minister Asquith.

The unexpected death of King Edward VII cast a pall over the country and left unsolved the controversy between the two houses of government. Churchill, however, was never a party politician; he saw two sides of a question and always chose a national or international viewpoint. He was never comfortable as a Conservative or a Liberal and did not fit either mold. The struggle to change the constitution lasted two years and Winston played an active part. It resulted in the supremacy of the House of Commons, the cornerstone of Winston's political faith, and has never yet been challenged.

In September 1908, Winston Churchill married Clementine Hozier, and in his words "lived happily ever after." He did not have an independent income nor was his bride well off, so they lived in modest circumstances. In 1910, he was named Home Secretary, and the next year offered the Admiralty which he accepted with alacrity. He was exuberant and regarded this his best chance. He had total fulfillment. He loved the sea and its romance and power, the dolphins and the turtles. "We have only the Navy," said the Prime Minister, as he offered Winston the position, "It is our only hope." Churchill was in his element.

Squabbles over unimportant matters arose and when they reached the Home Secretary's ears he threw himself into preparing for the worst. He was completely immersed from dawn to midnight day after day, taking no time off for relaxation. Trouble was brewing in Europe; Germany and Austria were aligned against France, Great Britain and Russia. It was 1912, and Germany passed a law authorizing that the Navy be kept in instant readiness for war. This prompted Churchill to further action. He mobilized the British Navy and joined with the French fleet moving ships to cover salient bases.

Winston was a man of thought and action. To him, they went together and he was never satisfied to plan a strategy and not take part in it. He and Lord John Fisher formed an air arm, the foundation of the Royal Air Force. Winston delighted in flying, his enthusiasm was limitless and he wanted the air force to be a part of the Navy so he established the Royal Naval Air Service.

By July 1914, the European struggle had gathered momentum. What should be the role of Britain? The government was divided, the House of Commons was divided, the country was divided. Germany asked for England's neutrality, the answer was No. Then Germany declared war on Russia, a country ill prepared for war. Germany failed to respect the neutrality of Belgium, Holland and France and invaded Belgium on August 4th. In defense of her neighbors, England declared war on Germany.

Churchill was fired to action. His day began at nine and went on until two the next morning. He was operating in three branches of defense—land, air and sea. Prime Minister Asquith appointed Lord Kitchener Secretary of State for War, and the British Navy set out to transport men to the mainland. But the war was not going well.

Churchill was sent to defend Antwerp, but too late and Antwerp fell, unleashing an attack on him by the press. Although the battle of the Marne was won, this did not assuage the criticism, and his enemies launched a campaign against his ability as head of the Admiralty. "What is the Navy doing? The Army is fighting and ships are being sunk." Winston could not tell them that the Navy was defending the coastline and transporting troops and supplies to France.

Winston Churchill had a passion for management and often breached lines of command, which the Prime Minister frowned upon and frayed nerves exacerbated. He was invaluable, however, and his ingenuity developed innovative implements of war, such as the armored car, the tank, and maneuvers that outwitted the enemy over and over again. His leadership dominated the atmosphere and he was admired by all except the few to whom he unwittingly emanated hostility.

Next came the campaign at Gallipoli, which was finally lost. The plan was to take the Dardenelles and proceed to Constantinople. Churchill felt the Navy could accomplish this without land troops, since Lord Kitchener could not spare any. Lord Fisher opposed these plans but was outnumbered and resigned as First Sea Lord. This caused a disruption, resulting in the formation of a Coalition Government. The disaster of Gallipoli rebounded on Churchill and he was ousted from the Admiralty. He was broken-hearted but determined to carry on in whatever position was granted him.

He was given a token ministry as Chancellor of the Duchy of Lancaster, but would be excluded from the War Council, so he resigned from Government and asked for active war service. Prime Minister Asquith considered his resignation a terrible waste of talent, for he had faith in Churchill's ability. Winston's speech of resignation before the House of Commons was brilliant and showed great restraint in the defense of his performance at the Admiralty, and he received a standing ovation.

Churchill left for the trenches in France, a Major in the Grenadier Battalion. His superior officers lost no opportunity to put him in his place and find fault with him, but it took only forty-eight hours for Winston to charm them with his good humor, his subservience and desire to learn, so the frosty reception soon thawed as he demonstrated that he was not only a "politician" but a soldier who could take orders. This was unusual behavior for Winston, but effectual in reaching his ends. He was so successful in winning over the Colonel that he gave Winston his command when he went on leave. A short while later, Churchill was put at the head of a battalion of the 6th Royal Scots

Fusiliers. This was a disappointment, as he relished the command of a brigade. However, he threw himself into the job with his usual vigor. He never did anything by halves.

His next move was auspicious. Home on leave, he spoke in the House of Commons as a member from Dundee, but without power, portfolio or backing. His speech caused consternation among his friends and criticism from his foes, when he strongly recommended the return of Lord Fisher to the Admiralty as First Sea Lord. The House was aghast and the press excoriated him. Those closest to him advised that he return to the front. He had left a sad regiment, all of whom respected and loved him and considered him a great man. They would "never have a commanding officer they liked half so well."

It was the third year of the war and things were not going well due to blundering by the War Office. Affairs at the Admiralty were also going badly and the Germans were forging ahead. Submarines decimated the British ships and at the battle of Jutland, Lord Kitchener seemed to have lost his nerve after the Dardanelles fiasco. It was evident that the situation required new leadership, a new perspective. Drastic changes took place, Prime Minister Asquith was replaced by Lloyd George and he appointed Churchill Minister of Munitions. Winston's duties were limited but he managed to impart to French leaders his "words of wisdom" regarding the handling of the war, many of which proved to be extremely successful. He rose early, worked until late morning then drove to the airport and hopped a plane to France; then back to his London office—no one the wiser.

When the United States entered the war, Churchill was put in charge of equipping the Americans, which he did so well that he was awarded the Distinguished Service Medal, the only Englishman to be so honored. The Armistice was declared on November 11, 1918 and Churchill's Popularity returned. He was finally recognized for his abilities and was offered two positions, Secretary of War and Secretary of Air, and turned to demobilization and the state of affairs in Russia, for the Revolution had left that country in chaos.

At this juncture, Winston's artistic talent emerged and tided him over a bad time when he was trying to find how he could best help his country. One of his military units commissioned an artist to do his portrait and Churchill was so intrigued that he bought the necessary tools and his natural talent blossomed.

In 1920, Churchill became Colonial Secretary and immediately turned his attention to Iraq where England maintained an army of occupation costing two hundred million dollars annually. He enlisted Colonel T. E. Lawrence, who had forsaken English society for the sands of Arabia, who ironed out the Iraqi difficulties, saving a hundred and sixty-five million dollars. After refusing a high Government office, Lawrence rode off across the desert into the sunset. Next, Churchill turned to Ireland and succeeded in having signed the Anglo-Irish treaty.

British politics continued to surge over whether to support Churchill or not. He was described as having great promise from the beginning of his career, but sometimes disappointed his friends, however, their faith in him was never destroyed. Winston was arrogant, at times impossible, yet lovable. His energy was prodigious and drained those around him. He had high intelligence, high drive and unusual courage and perseverance. He was fierce in his love and loyalties; for England, adventure, for politics and war. He had qualities of greatness but sometimes lacked discretion. He needed an ideal on which he could unleash his enthusiasm and forge ahead to achieve what in his view was good for mankind and the world.

In 1922, Winston's voice was stilled in the House of Commons when he lost the election at Dundee. His defeat was due partly to an attack of acute appendicitis which required surgery, and partly to the defeats at Antwerp and the Dardanelles. He was forty-seven and had tasted both success and failure. Where should he turn now?

After recuperating in Cannes, Winston put his energies into making a living, as his inheritance and royalties from his writings were not sufficient to support the high standards the Churchills maintained. Theirs was a happy family, with five children, one son, Randolph, and four daughters, one of whom died in her third year. Winston and Clemmie entertained a good deal, including as their guests men in public office upon whose wits Winston could sharpen his own. He had an idiosyncrasy about money, and spent much time and thought on how it came in but very little on how it went out. Consequently, Clemmie took over as much of the family's financial duties as Winston would allow.

Churchill began writing a history of the First World War entitled THE WORLD CRISIS, in four volumes. He worked long hours and sedentary life played heavily on his health. He did not look well, he was almost bald, stooped like a man of seventy and frightened Clemmie by his pallor. His physician was concerned but Winston would not listen to medical advice.

In 1923, Churchill was offered a candidacy at West Leicester but was defeated. He was caught between two ideologies, the old-line Conservatives whom he opposed and the emerging socialism in the Liberal and Labor parties of which he was suspicious. Where did he belong? He resigned from the Liberals and started a new party: the Constitutionalists. Then his friends persuaded him to stand from the constituency of Westminister in the heart of London, often called "the Washington of London," but he lost to the Conservatives. It was a moral victory, however, and a vote of confidence which boosted his morale.

Churchill's new stand stimulated the Conservative Party and everyone surmised that his Constitutionalists would join the Conservatives. In 1924, however, he was returned to Parliament by the constituency of Epping, and Prime Minister Stanley Baldwin named him Chancellor of the Exchequer. His Performance as Chancellor was notable for impulsiveness and lack of judgment and his tenure was anything but dull, for soon a Miner's Lockout was called, followed by a General Strike which Churchill set about breaking. As the newspapers were also on strike, he started the GAZETTE. With his brilliance and energy, he was too much for anybody, but because of his boisterous personality he was blamed for anything that went wrong. Baldwin epitomized him as having "a hundred horsepowered brain."

This was the ninth ministerial position Churchill had held—a record for Britain—and in 1929, he stepped down with a dazzling record, having made eight thousand speeches, fought five wars and become the most popular and the most unpopular man in England. Then he entered a ten-year period of retirement from the public eye referred to as the "lotus years."

Churchill, in disfavor by Government, resorted to speaking and writing and, after a lecture tour in the United States, busied himself with the reviews of THE WORLD CRISIS, and the favorable comments on his writings from authors, such as H. G. Wells, Sir Arthur Conan Doyle and John Masefield. He basked in the glow of these accolades while knocking off piece after piece for publication in magazines.

In 1935, Stanley Baldwin was again elected Prime Minister, but Churchill was passed over for a position, so he buried his disappointment in tackling the mammoth task of writing the history of his ancestor, the Duke of Marlborough, and appeased his boredom at the French Riviera where he regaled the guests at numerous dinner parties with his wit and brilliant discourse.

Winston always enjoyed a drink, and at this time his penchant for liquor threatened to run his life. "His drinking bouts were the talk of the Empire..." said Life Magazine, and his occasional speech in Parliament as a member from Epping was received with amusement as he pounded on the same old cry of the dangers of Socialism and the somnolence of Conservatism. One of his trademarks was his cigars. He was never seen without one stuck in his mouth. Sometimes it was lit, often not. Wherever he went he had to have his cigar, even in the bathtub, which he frequented twice each day. He went through a ritual for each of the sixteen he smoked every day, beginning with cutting off the end in what he considered the proper way, with a knife, never a cigar cutter.

In 1936, King Edward VIII shocked the world with his affair with Wallis Simpson and his desire to make her his wife. Edward and Winston had been buddies since Edward was Prince of Wales and he went to Churchill for counsel. Regardless of Winston's prophecies of success, King Edward chose abdication. Winston helped him draft his farewell speech.

Now came what some considered Winston's finest hour when he, alone of all Englishmen, took a stand against fascism. He finally persuaded his countrymen through his speeches and writings of the German danger; they had fallen into blissful somnolence, completely unaware, and the leaders were aging.. To Churchill, this was "mass blindness." He was the only one who could "see," the only one who had vision, but his warnings fell on deaf ears, and they remained deaf through Hitler's annexation of Poland, Czechoslovakia and Austria. On September 3, 1939, France and England declared war against Germany, and Churchill was called to resume his old post at the Admiralty. He strode into Commons amidst thundering applause—a short while ago he had been denounced—and set about picking up his duties.

Subsequent months brought tragedy to England in the sinking of many ships, but the sea war was merely a screen as the Germans prepared for the invasion. Then Norway fell and Holland awaited the coming blow. In the meantime, increasing dissatisfaction with the leadership of Neville Chamberlain reached the boiling point; his close friends suggested he step down, and King George asked Churchill to accept the position of Prime Minister—the answer to what Winston had strived for over many years. He was sixty-six years old. A few days later he delivered his memorable address on "blood, sweat and tears"—an immortal masterpiece.

With war came a threat to Churchill's personal safety, s' he called to duty his former bodyguard, Thompson. Theirs had always been a fine association, but there was many a time when Winston defied him during an air raid, remaining on the street so he could watch the bombs fall, or exiting from the shelter before they stopped. Several times he continued to enjoy his dinner alone, as bombs whistled by and buildings around him crashed down. He did not know what fear is and seemed to lead a charmed life.

Everyone in contact with Churchill felt the impact of his personality, his courage, his positive thinking and disregard of the possibility of disaster. His effect on those around him was almost hypnotic. His gift of insight and his powers of persuasion often turned the tide of defeat to victory. The rescue of 350,000 British and French soldiers from Dunkirk is an example. It was Churchill who ordered every seaworthy vessel from huge warships down to small pleasure boats to cross the channel, while the Royal Air Force protected the incongruous fleet on its mission to Dunkirk and back to England.

Churchill called a meeting of the Cabinet and outlined the realistic conditions of the war. Belgium had surrendered, France had fallen, and Russia had joined the Germans. "Gentlemen, we are alone," he said, "and I find it extremely exhilarating!" The most dire challenge was his greatest delight. Churchill let his colleagues know that he was in command; at no other time was his paranoia so apparent.

Winston was the hardest worker of the group, his hours extending to eighteen every day—his relaxation was watching "Deanna Durbin" movies. He had a wacky sense of humor and played harmless tricks on his associates if he disliked or found them undermining his authority. Especially when under tension, he resorted to buffoonery, and his doctors decided that he required this to ease the stress. Once, when a Cabinet member complained that he was asked to do two things at once with his right hand, Churchill stuck his thumb in his mouth, wiggled his fingers and exclaimed, "Look at my right hand—I am scratching my teeth and rubbing my nose at the same time!"

Churchill had a knack for making friends and won over leaders of countries important to England. He was a super salesman, delightful, engaging and a gracious host, who could charm the most recalcitrant to his political thinking. He thrived on danger—in fact, he welcomed it and was inclined to seek it out. To him, it was another challenge, which he was always on the lookout for.

The Battle of Britain began in July 1940. The Germans had abandoned the invasion of England and decided to bomb the island until it capitulated. By August, the R.A.F. had retaliated so successfully that Churchill delivered his famous speech; "Never in the field of human conflict was so much owed by so many to so few," but he was convinced that England needed help and America should enter the war. However, President Roosevelt and Ambassador Joseph Kennedy did not agree with him.

The Battle of Britain was waning, but the expectation of an invasion was ever present and each night the British expected troops to land by parachute. The war was not going well and Churchill, severely criticized, shouldered the blame. In January, Roosevelt sent his emissary, Harry Hopkins, to see Churchill. The United States was supplying Britain with arms and supplies on a pay as you go basis, but the time had come when Britain could no longer afford this, so in March, Roosevelt signed the Lend-Lease Bill. It was Hitler's death warrant.

In December, the Japanese bombed Pearl Harbor, involving the United States in a worldwide war. Churchill went to Washington to confer with President Roosevelt and on his return was greeted by a Parliament and a press urging his resignation. German propaganda claimed that he was unable to lead the country because of his drinking habits. Churchill addressed the House and demanded a vote of confidence. His speech was moving and he was very frank about the bad news and admitted that mistakes had been made and things were apt to get worse. His enemies wasted no time in placing the blame, but the vote was four hundred and sixty-four to one. Churchill expressed his determination that England would win the war.

Early in 1942, a London conference was held with the American delegates, and Churchill convinced them to agree to his program. The invasion of the continent was put on hold and that of West Africa embraced. Churchill went to Moscow to apprise Stalin of the plans and was accused of cowardice and deceit, but Stalin had no choice but to go along with the majority opinion. He was ungracious and insulting, but Churchill, with his usual adroitness, managed to assuage his attitude and they parted on fairly good terms.

General Montgomery broke through at last and defeated Rommel at Alamein in November 1942. Churchill was delighted that his controversial strategy had worked, and to add to his delight, American forces landed in West Africa, signaling the entry of the United States in the Second World War. According to Churchill, the end of 1942 was "the end of the beginning." He and Roosevelt met soon after and discussed whether to cross the English Channel and land in France, or to continue to go through Sicily and Italy. Churchill prevailed, and as it turned out, he was right. It was January 1944 and preparations were being made for the invasion of France. D-Day, June 6th, finally arrived. The next day Churchill addressed the House of Commons with the news that Rome had fallen, then described the taking of the beachheads in Normandie.

As the year rolled on, Roosevelt and his Generals had by now assumed full command of the war and Churchill had little influence over strategy. He continued to speak before the House but the quality of his oratory did not match that of four years ago. The relations between the two leaders were at their worst in December, when the Battle of the Bulge took place and was finally won on Christmas Day. Then on to Berlin and Hitler's demise. The historic Big Three Conference was held at Yalta and Churchill did not get his way and was irritable; Roosevelt was a sick man and Stalin wanted to get the talks over so he could proceed with his evil plans. The war was officially over on May 8th and at three o'clock, Churchill broadcast the news that Germany had surrendered unconditionally.

The next day, Churchill addressed the House of Commons and received an acclaim unsurpassed in its history. Shortly after, Franklin Roosevelt died, Harry Truman was President and, in June 1945, withdrew American troops from Russia. Churchill accepted this decision with reluctance, for he distrusted Stalin, sensed his intentions and feared the spread of Communism. His remarkable vision proved to be absolutely correct. In September 1945, the Americans dropped the bomb on Hiroshima and the Japanese capitulated.

A Big Three Conference was held at Potsdam, interrupted when

Churchill had to return to London for the General Elections. He was apprehensive as to the outcome and rightly so, for his Conservative Party was defeated and the Labor Party took office with Clement Atlee as Prime Minister. It was six years minus one day since Churchill took over, and he accepted his defeat with good grace; he was a good loser but it was extremely difficult for him. However, he had satisfied his ambition and reached his goal. He could climb no higher. The war was won. The world was indignant at his dismissal and presents began to arrive from every country, large and small.

Winston was not interested in honors and refused many without comment. It was said that he declined an English dukedom and the Order of the Garter, remarking: "Why should I accept the Garter from His Majesty when his people have just given me the boot?" Eight years later, however, he accepted it. He was content to bask in his achievements of which he was very proud, and on state occasions wore his full regalia, with the Order of the Garter, the Order of Merit and his many medals and ribbons on his left chest.

Through Winston Churchill's career ran a strong thread readily recognizable as paranoia, every aspect of which was manifest at some time during his life. His friends often remarked about his autocratic ways, such as hostility masked as sarcasm and his reluctance to acknowledge criticism. To him the opinions of others were not worth considering, and his innate compulsion to manage more often than not resulted in a one-man operation with things done his way, which he always considered to be the best. He made it very clear that it was he who was running the show. It was not easy working with Churchill, and drastic measures were at times required by his colleagues to deter him from what may have turned out to be a major blunder.

Winston interspersed his writing with various trips and, in 1946, went to the United States and received several honorary degrees. He chose Fulton, Missouri, sitting next to president Truman, for a speech expounding the growing hostility of Russia, the spread of Communism and the necessity of cementing Anglo-American relations. This warning had never yet been voiced worldwide and repercussions were widespread. Thus, Churchill ended his brilliant career in Government.

Winston Churchill's last eighteen years were spent writing, speaking before the house of Commons and traveling. He attended meetings of heads of state and filled his leisure time with painting, but his compulsion to write was paramount. Year after year he had published book after book. He was leader of the opposition in the House of Commons and in 1953 was made Knight of the Garter and awarded the Nobel Prize for literature. In 1959, he won his last election and in 1963 was made an honorary citizen of the United States, of which he was very proud.

Winston was fortunate in having Clemmie. She was the perfect wife for a man of his temperament, and enhanced his brilliant career without effacing her own individuality. He never looked at another woman. Unlike many great men, he was completely devoid of moral laxness. Although Winston's personality was flavored by his paranoid quality, he was a kind man, a gentle man, who loved children, animals and wild life and was devoted to his family and friends. His drinking was excessive, although he never appeared to be under its influence and always performed at his superlative level. Unlike Hitler and Stalin, he did not change at middle age from the individual dedicated to saving his country to the tyrannical dictators they became. No, he remained steadfast in his purpose—to save England and serve its people.

Churchill's mistakes were due to his overpowering conviction that he was right in his decisions, for his paranoia did not allow him to listen to others. He never, however, lost the admiration and love of the people who looked up to him as the savior of England and a genius unmatched by none. He will live in their hearts forever.

Winston was a little boy who never grew up. He enjoyed playing pranks and thrived on banter. He loved to talk and made no pretense at showing he was bored with chitchat, however, his audiences never tired of listening to him. He had several idiosyncrasies of which he was quite aware but was never embarrassed by them nor did he ever apologize for them. For instance, he was never on time and not concerned about it, and could not tolerate disorder of any kind, for he was a tidy person and apt to criticize one who was not.

His relaxation was watching movies—he had a few favorites—and playing cards, his favorite card game was bezique. During the Second World War, he had made what he called his "siren suit," which he donned when compelled to go into a shelter during an air raid. It was a loose-fitting garment zipped up the front. He loved hats of different shapes and kept a huge collection, donning the correct one for the occasion. He was autocratic and demanded attention, but at the same time was kind and thoughtful. He was subject to explosions due to frustration when small things went awry, but if an international crisis arose, he was calm and totally in control. He seemed impervious to stress, and did not know what fear is. "War is a game to be played with a smiling face," he said. He loved action and adventure, the "bright eyes of danger."

During the war, Churchill lived by a rigid schedule. He worked from six in the morning until eleven—in bed. Then he arose, dressed and saw his official people until one o'clock and from eleven in the evening until one in the morning. He lunched at one and slept from two until six in the afternoon. He saw people again until nine when he dined, and went to bed at two in the morning, after seeing his officials again. He kept six secretaries busy long hours and everyone around him hopping.

Winston's skill as an artist ranked as professional. He considered painting a therapeutic pastime, but soon realized it was more than that. He began in water colors then tried oils, which to his delight he thoroughly enjoyed and left a legacy of portraits and landscapes of vast proportions. He suffered four slight strokes and had two falls from which he recovered through sheer determination. During these later years, he used a cane and was slightly deaf, finally agreeing to a small hearing aid, which he turned off when bored.

Up to age eighty-seven, he refused help when walking, so he remained fairly active, traveling, attending meetings, dinners, and other affairs, and always the House of Commons. Rumors circulated that he was senile, but his thinking and speaking were clear until the end. His only complaint was that his legs would not carry him as he wished and his hearing was impaired. He made his last appearance in the House of Commons on July 27, 1964, four months before his ninetieth birthday and died peacefully of natural causes on January 14, 1965.

Winston Spencer Churchill was the greatest leader in war England has ever known. His record of accomplishment was tremendous, his genius to prognosticate and his energetic drive unmatched. He was a great statesman of heroic size, a giant among pygmies. His epitaph: courage, humor, pugnacity, love of people, love of life, and one of history's few benign paranoid dictators.

But if we look at Winston Churchill as being a benign paranoid, an exactly opposite stance must be taken for our next political leader.

NICOLAE CEAUSESCU

Nicolae Ceausescu was born January 26, 1918 in Scornicesti, Romania, the third son of a large peasant family. He dropped out of elementary school, and was apprenticed as a shoemaker. At fifteen he joined an illegal Communist youth group and in 1936 became a member of the party.

At the end of World War II, decisions made at the meeting at Yalta carved Europe into the Warsaw Pact, leaving some nations intact. Romania was consigned to Stalin and became a Communist country. Ceausescu rose quickly as the protege of the leader, Gheorghe Gheorghui-Dej who, on his death bed, designated Ion Georghe Maurer his successor. Maurer refused and suggested that the youngest man take over the leadership. That man was Ceausescu. Thus, in 1965, Nicolae Ceausescu was proclaimed President of Romania. He proceeded to establish the most efficient intelligence service in the world and to devise terrorist activities that reached over international boundries—the beginnings of an extreme paranoid dictator.

He then took steps to ensconce his wife, Elena, as vice-president and his two sons and daughter, his brothers and members of his family and friends in important positions. This was a first step in gaining control, for his ultimate goal was to be the leader of the Warsaw Pact. Clearly evident was his compulsive desire for widespread power, and his reach for self-aggrandizement was manifest in his efforts to become the most prominent member of the Soviet Union.

One of his objectives was to influence Western nations to regard Romania as the most favored nation of the Soviet bloc. Another was to gather on his side influential leaders with Communist leanings, so he established diplomatic and personal relationships with Moammar Gadhafi of Libya and Yasser Arafat of the Palestine Liberation Organization. The friendship of Arafat and Ceausescu flourished as they discovered one another's likes and dislikes and revelled in drinking, consuming mountains of food, indulging in pornography and sex. They were a conniving pair and one of their plots was the assassination of King Hussein of Jordan, whom they considered a menace to their aspirations.

In the late 1970s, Ceausescu, with Arafat and Gadhafi, became involved in the waves of terrorism near the time of the hijacking of the Achille Lauro and the planned assassination of Golda Meir, prime minister of Israel. Ceausescu foiled that attempt because he wanted to be the peacemaker between Egypt and Israel and be awarded the Nobel Peace Prize.

Early in his presidency, Ceausescu set about policing every Romanian citizen from the top official down to the lowly street cleaner. He had to know what they were doing, saying and thinking, for he was suspicious of everyone. Thus he could control their actions and be in total command. As is true of all dictators, Nicolae savored the power he wielded in being able to order the silencing of anyone who stood in his way, showed the slightest evidence of disloyalty or whom he disliked or did not trust. He despised all Hungarians, many of whom lived in Romania, and often, for no reason, they were targets of his ruthlessness. There were many people he wanted to eliminate, so he devised the code word "Radu," kill. He was known to use the word frequently.

Ceausescu's method of surveillance was to place microphones and tape recorders in every room where individuals might be working or relaxing, from the top executives down to the dishwashers, especially those in government. All were monitored without their knowledge. He and Elena had a particular fascination for the sex lives of their countrymen, and video cameras were placed in the bedrooms of certain persons, presumably to use the evidence for blackmail or as a means of coercion. Elena in particular relished watching the tapes.

Ceausescu established what was dubbed the "Horizon" operation, a widespread intelligence network that infiltrated the Western countries and was used to collect classified information and the latest technological knowledge. Both overt and covert, Horizon was instrumental in obtaining funds through devious means, one of which was to charge large sums of money to Germans and Jews desiring to emigrate to West Germany and Israel. Another project was the collection of money to provide orphaned children to Israeli and German couples. The money was received but the children were never delivered.

Horizon operation entailed the bugging of embassies, office buildings, private residences, public establishments and the recruitment of double agents as ambassadors, clergy, priests, bankers and other officials and professionals. Each agent was given a code word. This network extended from the United States to Africa, and Ceausescu personally handled it under the aegis of the DIE (Departmentul de Informati Externe), the equivalent of the KGB.

Microphones and tape recorders were everywhere; in bars and restaurants and bedrooms—even taxicabs. The constant recruiting of spies and double agents formed an endless web. Ceausescu stopped at nothing to obtain his ends; for example, one agent who worked as a driver for the American Ambassador, developed an affair with the Ambassador's wife and obtained information that she had gotten from her husband. Ceausescu had built a secret room in which an electronic system was set up so he could monitor the thousands of microphones and tape recorders and listen in on any location. This was his key to power and control and he gleaned information from this enormous lattice work that enabled him to purge the Politburo and, indeed, entire Romania of all but his supporters. He was heard to say: "Microphones are the most efficient intelligence weapons there are."

What sort of man was Nicolae Ceausescu? Physically, he was short of statue and square of build. He was egocentric, cruel, conniving, suspicious and thought nothing of using people to gain his ends. Power was his goal and he paid little attention to the well-being and needs of others. He was a gourmand and drank heavily—Johnny Walker Black Label was his favorite Scotch Whiskey, of which he imbibed frequently and often in excess. Since his rise to power, he never touched money, but spent lavishly on clothes, expensive automobiles, anything he wanted. The state paid for everything.

Neither he nor Elena wore a piece of clothing more than once; suits, coats, dresses, underclothing, everything was discarded. Then, all was burned. As they wore only the most expensive clothes, the amount of money wasted was considerable. Nicolae was fanatically afraid of being poisoned or physically hurt. He was paranoid to an excessive degree in this and would never put to his lips food or drink unless the servant who prepared it tasted first. His table manners were atrocious, he ate with his hands, and smeared food and spilled drink over his clothes. When he shook hands, he washed them with alcohol. He was terrified of "germs."

As for Elena, she was of similar type—excessively paranoid. However, she bowed to Nicolae's will in matters of state but was overbearing and authoritative when it came to her own interests. She claimed to be a scientist, her major field was chemistry—but the authenticity of her claim was in doubt, however, under the aegis of her husband's iron hand she usually got her way. It appears that she was able to assuage his sexual appetite, which may have had a bearing on their compatibility. At any rate, she was self-centered, demanding, domineering, uncaring and totally oblivious of the needs and wants of others. Elena was fond of expensive jewelry, and had the best jewelers bring their wares to her. She chose many pieces but never sent one back.

As Elena wormed her way into power, she traveled with her husband from one country to another, demanding acclaim, degrees, memberships in prestigious societies, diplomas and so forth. She expected and received expensive presents of jewelry, furs, mink coats and silver, while Nicolae had his choice of the best automobiles. Elena was convinced of her scientific "genius" and promoted a book on science she claimed she wrote. In reality it was written by a group of scholars she never met. She was considered by some more heartless and cruel than her husband and poured sarcasm and scorn on all with whom she came in contact.

As a couple, their favorite entertainment was home movies. Nicolae liked Kojak films and they both were partial to pornographic pictures. They topped off the evenings with a snack of tomatoes, onions and feta cheese accompanied by Nicolae's scotch whiskey and Elena's champagne.

The Ceausescus had two sons and a daughter. The oldest, Valentin, was adopted, and when he married the daughter of a former opponent, Nicolae disowned him. Zoia was under her mother's thumb, but refused to marry the men her mother chose, so she soon left home. Nicu, the youngest, was the only one who accepted his father's policies and was rewarded by being placed in influential positions. in which his performance was inferior. Nicu was a drunken, spoiled brat, a full-time playboy and a disgrace to his parents. They paid no attention, however, and condoned everything he did.

The Ceausescus were obsessed with diamonds, and built a synthetic diamond plant as a gift to Nicolae on his 60th birthday. They planned to sell diamonds to Western Europe as another way of raising money to put into their Swiss and other foreign bank accounts. Nicolae kept a firm hold on the accounting system of the government and manipulated the percentages to reflect what he wanted seen, as he unashamedly skimmed the cream off the top of the Treasury and hid it. At this point he had amassed so much wealth that he had built an underground vault in his mansion that could hold four hundred million dollars in cash.

Although plans for the trip to the United States dominated Ceausescu's days, he delegated his staff to carry them out in order to take care of pressing needs at home. First, he ordered the creation of bacteriological and chemical weapons the day after they were banned by an international appeal for their abolition. He then became engaged in disposing of all men and women who were of less than two generations of Romanian descent, and proclaimed that only Romanians could hold office and only Romanians could marry. In order to carry out these evil intentions, he used his code name "Radu." Many innocent people were thus summarily executed.

Ongoing were the extensive operations of the DIE, including the selling of counterfeit passports, both American and Western, many taken from dead Arabs. Wheeling and dealing in oil, for which was charged an exorbitant price, planning terrorist attacks and so forth occupied Nicolae's days. Western countries were asked to bid on building factories, then he cancelled the work after having photographed the schematics and technical information. When expedient, Nicolae sold this to other countries in the Warsaw Pact. And from each source he extracted his "pound of flesh" to be salted away in his bank accounts.

One of Nicolae Ceausescu's top priorities was to cement friendly relations with neighboring countries and the Western world, so he had his people plan one trip after another. He visited Moscow and met with Brezhnev, whom he disliked and suspected was plotting against him, but paid homage out of deference to his position. Brezhnev showed him the Soviet version of the United States' Strategic Defense Initiative, and gave him electronics technology stolen from Texas Instruments and Fairchild Corporation.

He met with Willy Brandt of West Germany, Ferdinand Marcos of the Philippines, and again with Yasser Arafat and Moammar Gadhafi. He learned about weapons systems, intelligence, strategic defense, anti-ballistic missile systems, computer technology and military hardware. Ceausescu gloated that the Soviet Union and Romania had enough intelligence capability to wrest from the United States the information necessary to disarm the West. He became euphoric over the mere contemplation!

He approached President Charles de Gaulle of France and received technical knowledge of microelectronics and computer software. Then, he ingratiated himself with Pakistani's Ali Bhutto with whom he worked out an arrangement to exchange intelligence information to their mutual benefit. In all these deals, his objective was to get something for nothing. His policy was never to pay for anything he wanted, but to steal it. He stole technology from the United States, West Germany, France, and Italy, on steel, metal alloys, aluminum, integrated circuits, electronics, computer equipment, medicines and drugs.

As time went on, Ceausescu's paranoia increased. One of his bête noir was Radio Free Europe broadcasting Western propaganda to Romania. He gave it the code name "Chatterbox" and ordered the Securitate to identify all who listened. When this could not be monitored, he flew into a rage and imposed another rule: to obtain a sample of handwriting from every citizen and match it to letters written to the station. Then do away with the writers. He decreed that all mail to and from the West be censored, and every typewriter registered with the military and none bought without its permission. Thus, a reign of terror was established throughout the land and the order "Radu" was more feared than ever.

Another manifestation of paranoia was the bugging of the Athenee Palace Hotel where visiting dignitaries stayed. It was a virtual intelligence factory; monitoring devices in every room, in the ashtrays and flower vases and in the bathrooms. There were concealed television cameras throughout and agents disguised as guests and hotel employees everywhere; even the call girls were spies.

Ceausescu was particularly afraid of defectors, afraid they would tell his story to the western world, so the DIE was instructed to keep an eagle eye out for anyone who talked about leaving the country. When told of such a case: "Radu!"

Now Ceausescu focused his attention on his trip to the United States during the administration of Jimmy Carter. He had already met Presidents Nixon and Ford and conjectured that President Carter, for whom he had little respect, would be more vulnerable. So he planned carefully by planting agents about Atlanta and at Carter's peanut farm. He instructed an agent to cosy up to the minister of the President's church and relate the incidents of civil rights that are afforded the Romanian people—all lies. He had agents posted in Washington, gathering information pertinent to his visit.

The Ceausescus travelled with everything they might need. They were to reside at Blair House and Nicolae gave extensive orders for its preparation; it was examined for electronic surveillance; radiation detectors were installed and every room was guarded around the clock. The walls were washed down with disinfectant by Ceausescu's people and the floors scrubbed. They brought their own sheets and towels and other such necessities. They did not trust anyone. They brought their food and had their meals in their rooms. Again, they ate nothing until one of the servants tasted it. Nicolae never touched the food at state dinners, but disposed of it under the table.

In April 1978, Nicolae Ceausescu and Elena were met at the airport by Cyrus Vance, then Secretary of State. Nicolae was miffed that the President was not there. When they had their first meeting with President and Mrs. Carter, the band played the old Romanian anthem instead of the one adopted by Ceausescu, who was furious and scowled as he stood at attention. As is the custom in this country, Rosalyn Carter gathered the wives together for trips and luncheons. Elena resented this as she wanted to be in on the affairs of state with her husband. Furthermore, she disliked women and felt she was superior to them. Frustrated, she resorted to complaining about everything and making herself a general nuisance.

Ceausescu ordered his staff to prepare his speeches and to include lavish and elaborate praises for him and Elena and accounts of the civil liberties the Romanians enjoy back home. He instructed that they quote Romanian emigres in the United States complimenting his management of Romanian affairs. He was always on the watch for devious means to gain his ends and his methods of manipulation were unparalleled. He tried to engage Billy Carter, the President's brother, as an agent by bribing him. He persuaded the Mafiosi to eliminate defectors from Romania, including Laszlo Hamos, who organized the demonstrations in New York during his visit, which sent him into a violent rage.

Ceausescu visited Texas Instruments in Dallas and the NASA installation at Houston, then on to New Orleans where he negotiated the procurement of an off shore drilling rig to be sent to Romania. Then the Ceausescus went to New York where noisy demonstrations took place outside the Waldorf Astoria where they stayed. This infuriated Nicolae and he demanded the President to order the demonstrators killed! On their return to Romania, Nicolae and Elena were met by thousands of citizens rejoicing at their safe arrival in Bucharest—all staged by staff. The newspapers were replete with releases flattering them—all written on Nicolae's orders.

Ceausescu's next mission was to Yugoslavia to meet with President Tito and cement their friendship. They were birds of a feather and had a grand time drinking heavily and enjoying themselves on Tito's yacht. Nicolae decided he too should have a yacht, so he sent an emissary to Greece to buy Aristotle Onassis' "Christina." Tito had two Rolls Royces, so Nicolae wanted two also, which he would buy on his trip to London. The two plotted together. Nicolae kidnapped three Yugoslavs Tito wanted out of the way and in return Tito kidnapped a Romanian political opponent who had emigrated to France.

Ceausescu's goal was to raise Romania to second place in the Warsaw Pact and create an arms industry for exportation independent of Moscow. His strategy had two parts, to manufacture arms for Romania and the Warsaw Pact, and to export arms to the Third World. Together, he and Tito could defeat the West and capitalism. By 1982, Romania was the fifth largest exporter of arms in the world, but at great sacrifice of its people.

In 1986, Ceausescu, never satisfied, planned to build a magnificent presidential palace for himself and Elena in Bucharest. To make space, he ordered the demolition of thousands of old dwellings and public monuments, hospitals, churches, monasteries and landmark sites. The press retaliated but Ceausescu fought back, claiming lies and treachery. Word of this destruction was broadcast and the world was aghast. But what the world did not know was what Ceausescu was doing to the Romanian people.

The people shivered in winter while Nicolae exported the oil and pocketed the money. "Radu" was in force and the killings went on, terrifying the populous. His will was law as he signed his name ordering this and decreeing that, even requiring that all women bear no fewer than four children.

Over Ceausescu's twenty-four year reign, food became more and more scarce, and most items were rationed. Although the country was agriculturally productive, much that was produced was exported to pay the foreign debt and the people went hungry. Ceausescu established the "nomenclatura," or elite class. It was the privileged superstructure of the people consisting of the heads of state and others designated by Ceausescu and Elena who, with the DIE, supervised its administration. Its members were recognizable by the cars they drove and their level of rank by color—black Mercedes and Rolls-Royces for the Ceausescus, down to white inexpensive cars for the lowest officer. They were known by the houses they lived in, the restaurants they ate in, the stores and public places they frequented and so forth, all paid for by the government and off limits to the people. The rest of the population muddled along with inferior goods, shortages of food and other necessities, poor medical care and long lines for all services.

In December 1989, a demonstration took place in Timisoara against Ceausescu's tyranny. Thousands died as the Securitate (secret police) rushed in to quell the movement. Ceausescu had given the order to kill "anyone who does not obey orders should be shot" as troops were sent in to suppress the demonstrators. But it was the beginning of Ceausescu's downfall. The people had enough and were ready to sacrifice their lives to be rid of him.

Ceausescu, always arrogant, and assured that his order would frighten the people to submission, took off for a three day trip to Iran. On his return, he called for a gathering of the people in the square. As he began to speak, the people, who numbered in the thousands, booed and shouted for freedom from oppression. Unaccustomed to opposition, he stepped back as the crowds booed him, a stunned look on his face—a sign to the people that their leader was vulnerable. Unnerved, he stopped speaking and left the podium with his wife. Two days later. they escaped by helicopter from the roof of the Central Committee building only to be apprehended by Ceausescu's own men. A provisional government was quickly formed and Nicolae Ceausescu, the last hard-line Communist leader in the Warsaw Pact, and his wife, Elena, were tried and convicted of genocide and "grave crimes" against Romania at a secret military trial and executed by firing squad. It was Christmas Day 1989.

A REVIEW OF DIFFERENCES 11

Let's review the similarities and differences between these paranoid personalities. First, how are they alike? One, they all chose vocations that afforded them access to large numbers of people. Second, they were highly intelligent with the exception of Idi Amin Dada, about whom it is rumored that he tested positive for syphilis, which may account for a semblance of mental disorder never diagnosed.

All these personalities were more doers than thinkers, completely egocentric and even the benign had little regard for other people. They also possessed high energy which provided them with the drive to forge ahead, ignoring those who interfered with their plans.

In addition, the personality attributes of paranoia were present in each: suspiciousness, the inability to accept criticism, the unshakable conviction that they were always right and that the ideas of others were not worthy of consideration. And most importantly, they were possessed with the compulsion to control all situations and persons within their purview. They revelled in haranguing the masses with the purpose of winning them over, then to control them, for the paranoid's one goal is to control, manipulate and accumulate wealth and possessions, thus gaining power over all.

So our "case" paranoids had many traits in common. Now let's discuss the differences of each. With the exception of Idi Amin Dada, all started out doing good deeds, thus gathering around them the masses of people they were out to control. Once accomplished, the malignant group slowly reversed, and total disregard for others and their well being replaced the benevolent spirit which heretofore had been the overriding purpose, like white turning to black, good to evil.

Although extremely paranoid, John Noyes was a good man. He had a vision which he translated into reality. He persuaded a number of people to join his group and they all lived happily for a number of years. John Noyes made strict rules and dictated how his flock should act, and saw to it his orders were obeyed.

John Pierpont Morgan was also a good man who thought only of what in his opinion was best for his country. His insatiable drive prompted him to establish single handed the financial community in the United States. He was a formidable character, his way was the right way and those who opposed him soon found they were no match for

him, and he prevailed in every project he undertook. He was dictatorial in family matters and saw to it that his wife and children obeyed
his wishes. His paranoia only became distressingly apparent near the
end of his life as failing health caused him to be irritable and difficult.

John Edgar Hoover was a benign dictator. All his life he fought
for what he considered was best for his beloved country. He created
the most efficient and effective investigative organization in the world
and staffed it with high-principled and honest men and women. He
was a controlling person but only over his Bureau, and withstood the
onslaughts of the political arena ethically and honorably. Only at the
end of his life when he had to defend his position, did his paranoia
develop into hostility and over-suspicion.

John Patterson was an empire builder who made his mark on the
manufacturing community. He was considerate of other people but
authoritative and domineering as he built up his business. He was an
asset to the community and gave generously of his money to those in
need. In business, however, he was autocratic and commanding of his
top management. Near the end of his career he began to act unreasona-
bly and got into trouble with the law.

So far, these individuals were outstanding and honorable men,
each of whom made a significant mark on his community or country.
They possessed a benign type of excessive paranoia that was never
inherently cruel or wicked. We move now into the next category
whereby the individual begins with fine intentions but deteriorates
into a malevolent, pernicious type of personality.

Aimee Semple McPherson was an evangelist of superior quality
and started her career with excellent intentions. She was a forceful
speaker and her preaching brought in millions of dollars which she put
to good works. This went on for many years but at midlife, Aimee
became worldly, neglected her responsibilities and abandoned her
mother who had helped her all along. Her paranoia became apparent
and her morals unacceptable, not becoming a minister of the gospel.
She refused to listen to advice and spent the Temple money on
frivolous activities and expensive cars, furs and clothes, as well as
many trips around the world with a male companion, presumably
preaching the gospel.

For most of her reign as prime minister, Indira Nehru Gandhi
appeared to be a benign dictator, working for the independence of her
country. She kept a tight reign over the members of her cabinet, and
those who worked for her found her difficult, as she was extremely
opinionated and manipulated her staff. Her paranoia was exacerbated
when, under siege by the opposition, she declared an emergency
which amounted to virtual dictatorship and absolute power. Then the
cruelty began. She professed no knowledge of this, but brutal acts were
continued by her orders, presumably against her wishes. Her dictator-

ship ended with her assassination.

Huey Long knew what he wanted in life when he was young—control and power. He won the governorship of Louisiana by campaigning for the people and did much good for the state. He manipulated his way until he was the virtual dictator of Louisiana. His cruelty manifested itself in vicious attacks on the Senate Floor and in the speeches he made while campaigning. He was aspiring to the presidency when he was assassinated.

Jim Jones' personality turned around quickly. His preaching promised a better life and he amassed a following of several hundreds. He tricked his flock into contributing their money and possessions and coerced some by having them beaten before the group. The psychological and physical cruelty he administered was heartless and brutal. When he was about to be investigated in Guyana, he staged a mass murder suicide and nine hundred people died.

We will discuss Nero, Mengistu and Idi Amin Dada together as they are similar in personality, and showed excessive cruelty from early adulthood on. Thus they differ from the others. Nero began by poisoning his brother and murdering several members of his family as well as anyone who stood in his way to power and control. Mengistu installed himself as dictator of Ethiopia by torture and bloodshed after toppling the regime of Haile Selassie. His grab for power and frenzy to control resulted in torture and execution without trial of hundreds of thousands of Ethiopians and millions faced starvation from the drought because he side-tracked the food sent from all over the world to alleviate the suffering.

Idi Amin Dada grew up in an atmosphere of witchcraft and showed signs of cruelty and desire for control early in life. He cheated and lied and murdered for control and power, and was totally oblivious of the feelings of others. The type of brutality he forced upon his fellow Ugandans is unprecedented and he finally was run out of the country. There are rumors that he is planning a coup to regain power and be reinstated as ruler.

Josef Stalin was rebellious and dictatorial as a child, and at a young age he joined Lenin who helped further his career and by the time he was forty-five he was the virtual ruler of the Soviet Union. He changed Lenin's policies and instituted his own, but had opposition from members of the Politburo so eliminated them one by one. Then he conducted an internal purge and eradicated most members of the cabinet, officials and army officers. He made himself the military leader, premier and generalissimo. From the beginning of his career his paranoia was evident and he played a large part in transforming Russia into what it is today.

Adolf Hitler's extreme paranoia was apparent from early childhood. He dropped out of school at sixteen and spent the next few years in useless activity. He served in the first world war after which he went into politics and planned his dream that Germany conquer Europe, annihilate the Jews and he would be "Master of the World." He formed a small group and step by step rose to power and the German people were ready for him after their defeat which left the country politically and socially destitute. His grandiose paranoid tendencies were in full flower. He then proceeded to carry out his plan of world domination which caused the annihilation of millions of innocent people and unbelievable destruction.

Winston Churchill was a great leader with an uncommon list of accomplishments and, as we've said, one of history's few benign paranoid dictators. His career displays the true benefits, under the right conditions, of paranoia.

And our last case, Nicolae Ceausescu, points to the horrifying results of the extreme paranoid personality run rampant—the entire world seemed relieved at his forced departure from this earth.

GLOBAL PARANOIA: ON THE RISE OR WANE?

12

C ontrolling, ambitious and hypersensitive people have the makeup we describe as paranoia. How long have they been with us? Hippocrates was the first to describe the paranoid trait and, as primitive man walked the earth thirty thousand years ago, paranoia protected him and contributed to his survival. Drawings and artifacts unearthed by archaeologists reveal his aggression, so there is no doubt that paranoia has been with us since the beginning of mankind.

Early man found ways to provide for his basic needs: food, shelter and clothing. Those who were born with excessive paranoia demanded more of life and challenged neighbors for their possessions and then, not satisfied, pressed on to expand into the next village, and the next and the next. They drove on until they won, widening the control of more and more territory, or until they overextended and collapsed.

Paranoid masters acquired possessions, enslaving those with lower energy and little paranoia to do their bidding.

When the revolutions began, the agricultural first, then the technological and the electronic, leading to the nuclear age we are in today, with the ability to destroy mankind and all living things, the paranoid people created more and eradicated more than ever before. Thus, primitive men evolved to the sophisticated human beings we are today, struggling for survival but with those eternal paranoids in charge.

The evolution of civilization is based on the premise that excessive paranoid personalities developed in every culture and became leaders with the compulsion to control and to wield power, the driving force of their makeup. They were restive, self-seeking, aggressive, ambitious empire builders, born with talents and skills by which they built civilization step by step, and from these efforts much has taken place through the millennia, extreme paranoids leading the way, some good and some evil. Some formed the building blocks of civilization as it evolved; several caused great suffering and the untimely death of millions of innocent people, and others brought about both. Self-aggrandizement is part of the paranoid personality and vast accomplishments contribute to the enhancement of ego, so they proceeded to build cities and waterways and highways, using the rest of the population as soldiers and slaves to accomplish this. Some leaders were good and great men, some wicked and cruel, but all possessed tremendous drive and high intelligence. Their achievements remain evident today. It is clear that excessive paranoia contributed enormously to the evolution of man.

Two hundred years ago, the world's youngest country established a democracy, providing freedom for its people for the first time in history. When that democracy was barely a hundred years old, countries of the western world followed suit and others were close behind, forming democracies, although painfully and slowly for some. Most remarkable of all, for the first time since the rise of Stalin, Russia has espoused glasnost and peristroika and the new openness allows citizens freedom to travel and communicate without fear of reprisal.

This Russian metamorphosis precipitated the toppling of dictators in Eastern Europe one by one and events are moving so fast there is no chance of retribution on the part of the despots who have fallen before massive peaceful demonstrations by the people. Is this new found freedom merely a passing phase? No, the people have spoken, and where tyranny still rules they are organizing quietly, as one nation after another awakens to the call for liberty and freedom.

The European nations are forming a community and working toward common goals. There is a growing consciousness of the interdependence of all nations and of all life, resulting in slow but steady progress towards unity, acceptance and understanding of all races, creeds and colors of peoples. Thus, paranoid personalities whose intentions are evil cannot have the same power or control, for they are blocked by the openness of society and the infiltration of information by the media revealing their plans and purposes. The world has become an open book and we ponder, what next?

In his frenetic search for more knowledge, better machines, new discoveries, man continues to invent, research and develop. He has conquered space, reached the moon and is planning to visit other planets. Should we question what these achievements proved? Indeed, what next?

How did all this come about? We give credit to Michail Gorbachev for his role in putting the heat on the cold war and opening the windows of Russia to allow the fresh air of freedom to blow in. Has the threat of nuclear destruction brought the world to its senses? Have we reached the climax of hate and destruction and begun the descent into peaceful coexistence? Is global paranoia increasing or taking another direction? Or is it waning so the battered world can be at peace at last?

One thing is for certain: paranoid people will survive and continue to exert their particular pressures on the rest of us. Let's hope it is for better rather than for worse.

THE END